## A BEAUTIFUL MESS

# HAPPY
# Handmade
# HOME

# A BEAUTIFUL MESS
# HAPPY
# *Handmade*
# HOME

## PAINTING, CRAFTING, AND DECORATING A CHEERFUL, MORE INSPIRING SPACE

**FROM THE CREATORS OF A BEAUTIFUL MESS**

*Elsie Larson* AND *Emma Chapman*

POTTER STYLE
New York

**For our father,**
the handiest man we know

Published in the United States by Potter Style, an imprint of Crown Publishing Group, a division of Penguin Random House LLC, a Penguin Random House Company, New York.

www.potterstyle.com

www.crownpublishing.com

POTTER STYLE and colophon are registered trademarks of Random House LLC.

Library of Congress Cataloging-in-Publication Data

Larson, Elsie, author.
  A beautiful mess happy handmade home : a room-by-room guide to
painting, crafting, and decorating a cheerful, more inspiring space /
Elsie Larson and Emma Chapman.
     pages cm
  ISBN 978-0-7704-3405-2 (paperback)—ISBN 978-0-7704-3406-9 (ebook
edition)
1.  Handicraft. 2.  House furnishings.
3.  Interior
decoration--Amateurs' manuals.
I. Chapman, Emma, author. II. Title.
  TT157.L255 2014
  745--dc23

2014008902ISBN 978-0-7704-3405-2
eISBN 978-0-7704-3406-9

Printed in China

Design by Jenny Kraemer

Photography by Janae Hardy

Cover design by Jenny Kraemer

Cover photograph by Janae Hardy

# *Contents*

Introduction 9

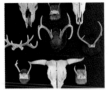

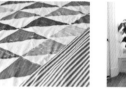

# *Introduction*

Hi there! We're Elsie and Emma and we are so happy you decided to pick up our book.

Over the past few years we've purchased our first homes and decorated them from the smallest corners to the biggest spaces. Before we started working on our homes, our blog, A Beautiful Mess, was mostly small crafts (think pillows and hair clips). If you had told us that someday we'd be building tables and making rugs and painting for fun on Friday nights, we would have laughed. Turns out, we got addicted.

A few years later, our homes look and feel nothing like they did the day we got our keys. They look like us now. Weird? Maybe. Cool? We'd like to think so. Personal? For sure. Personality is the most important aspect of decorating for us. Who cares if your house is nice if your friends and family can't see *you* in every room?

This book was born from the pure joy that big décor projects brought into our lives. It's special. We're geeky, but we'd even call it life changing. We hope you get the same goose bumps from your first giant DIY project (spoiler alert—you totally will).

## A FEW TIPS FOR YOUR JOURNEY

Don't be afraid to mess up.
We know it's a giant cliché to say "there's no right or wrong" and "you have to break the rules sometimes," but it's SO true. We made our fair share of mistakes and regrets from our home projects—but rest assured, it's all fixable! Once we were trying too hard for a "classic" design and the result was a boring dining room. Good news—mistakes happen. Often the best lessons are learned when we go with plan B because the first idea was a big fail. No matter how awesome you are, you'll mess up sometimes. Go with it!

Our ideas are only starting points.
The ideas in this book are specific to us. We photographed almost everything in our two homes this year. Think beyond

the projects we share and find ways to make them your own! We know you're creative, so don't feel limited by what's found within these pages—use it as a jumping-off point to express your personality in your space! As long as you start a project after you put down this book, we've played our part.

If you love it, *love it*.
Whether an idea seems trendy, obvious, awful, or even (gasp!) overdone, we encourage you to stop caring about what other people think. The point of decorating is to make your home more *you*. At the end of the day the only thing that matters is how you feel in your home. Does it help you unwind? Does it make you smile? We encourage you to create a space that caters only to you and the loved ones in your home. How sad would it be to invest all this time and money into your personal space, only to create a cookie-cutter something that doesn't hold meaning for you? Trust yourself. Create a home that feels like you in the big ways and the tiny details.

## READY, SET, GO!

Are you craving change in your décor? Are you slightly excited, but also a little nervous to try a big idea in your home? Here are a few questions to jump-start the process. We answered all of these while designing rooms for this book, and you have no idea how many lightbulb moments we had. We hope you do too!

*1.* List all your favorite spaces (homes you love, but also hotels, restaurants, retail stores, etc.). In the next column, list everything you admire about each place. What were you doing there? Did you like the smells and the music? What features stood out to you? How did that space make you feel? How would you describe the style of these rooms? Take your time—really think about your answers. When I made my list I was shocked by how the spaces I loved visiting contrasted from the spaces I usually pin on Pinterest. You might surprise yourself too!

**2.** List the activities you envision doing in each room. Sure, a dining room will be used for eating, but what else? Will you play cards with friends, share a bottle of wine, host a romantic dinner or a silly reality TV-themed party? Think about all the members of your household and how they will use the room. We firmly believe that rooms should be designed for living.

**3.** Choose colors that make you feel something. For now, don't worry about what colors go in each room—that's not the point. List all of the colors that you have a strong reaction to and how they make you feel, whether it is positive, negative, or a mixed emotion. List what the colors remind you of. List colors that you've loved in rooms, movies, or inspiring artwork.

**4.** This next one might be slightly embarrassing, but please go there with us! Make a list of 100 things about YOU. Things you love, quirks, aversions, memories, dreams, and little details that make you one of a kind.

Now that you've created these giant lists (they'd better be giant!), save them in the back of your book until you've finished reading. When you're done, go through each list with a highlighter and pick out anything that could serve as inspiration for your new space!

We can't wait to see what you create in your homes! Please keep in touch with us via our blog, abeautifulmess.com, and send us photos of your projects. We would love to see them!

If you need us, we'll be at home trying more projects. We weren't kidding when we said we are addicted!

XO,

*elsie + emma*

# LIVING
# ROOMS
_____

***Whether you're drinking*** your morning coffee or coming home after a rough day, your living room should make you light up. It should be a place that invites games and naps and parties. There are no rules except this—*make it your own*. Challenge yourself to unlearn everything you ever knew about decorating. Erase every rule. Open up your mind to the endless ways to customize your space and make it feel like *your* cool place.

In this chapter you'll see our polar opposite but equally party-worthy living rooms. We're constantly rearranging and reimagining our spaces. If we had stuck to design rules, Emma never would have chosen to paint all her walls black and I surely wouldn't have picked out a bright yellow couch. Moral of the story: *it's all good*! Our spaces reflect our personalities and inspire us to invite guests into our homes.

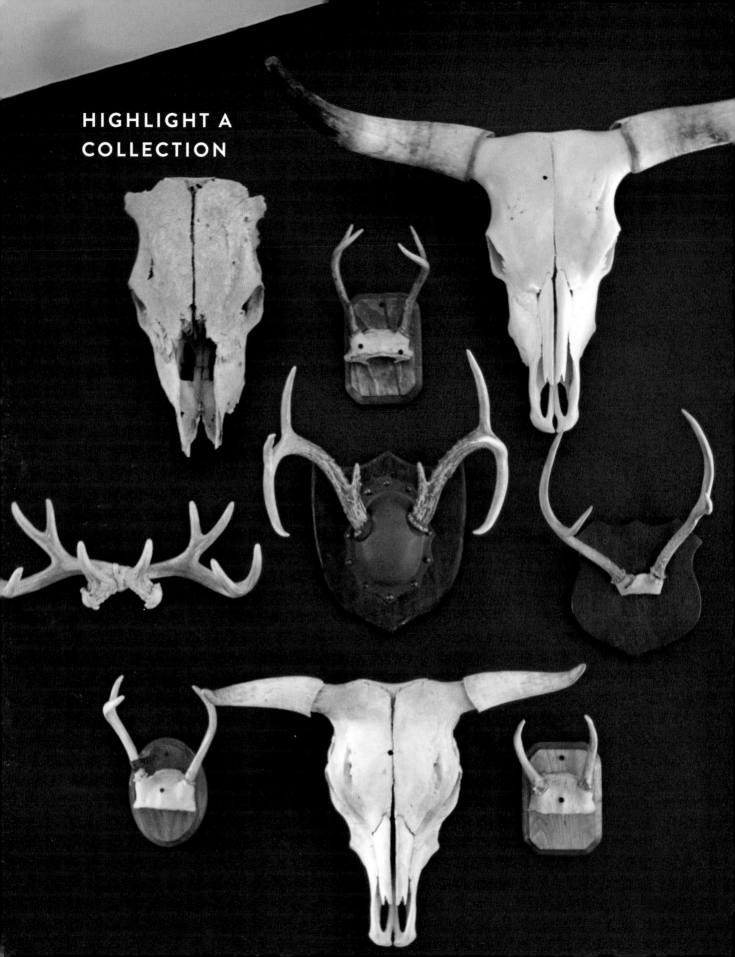

We all have possessions or collections we are proud of and cherish. Prominently displaying these items can add personality to your living room. Try hanging a collection of antlers on one wall or building/buying a special display case to house your cat figurine collection. Whatever items make your heart flutter— show them off!

# PATTERNED COFFEE TABLE

Are you lusting over fancy patterned-wood tables? If you can't find the perfect one for your space, consider making your own by covering an inexpensive table with balsa wood.

### SUPPLIES

Ikea coffee table

black acrylic paint

rags

balsa wood

wax paper

3 different wood stains

scissors

wood glue

polyurethane

**1.** Paint the top and sides of your coffee table with the black acrylic paint and let dry (this will make any gaps pieces less noticeable).

**2.** Stain the balsa wood in three colors to cover a rectangle of 16 by 30 inches in the middle of your coffee table (or however big your table is).

**3.** Once your stain has dried, use scissors to cut triangles 4 inches tall and 5 inches wide. Arrange the triangles to fit the 16-by-30-inch space using half triangles at the beginning and end of each row.

**4.** Use wood glue to secure each triangle to the coffee

table and place a heavy, flat object on top while the glue dries to prevent curling.

**5.** Stain enough balsa wood to cover the rest of the top and sides of the coffee table.

**6.** Cut pieces to lengths needed and make sure to angle the corner cuts for the top. Create a pattern out of paper if you need one.

**7.** Glue the pieces in place and, again, set heavy items on the wood as it dries.

**8.** Use 1 to 2 coats of polyurethane to seal the wood once your glue is dry.

*d.i.y.*

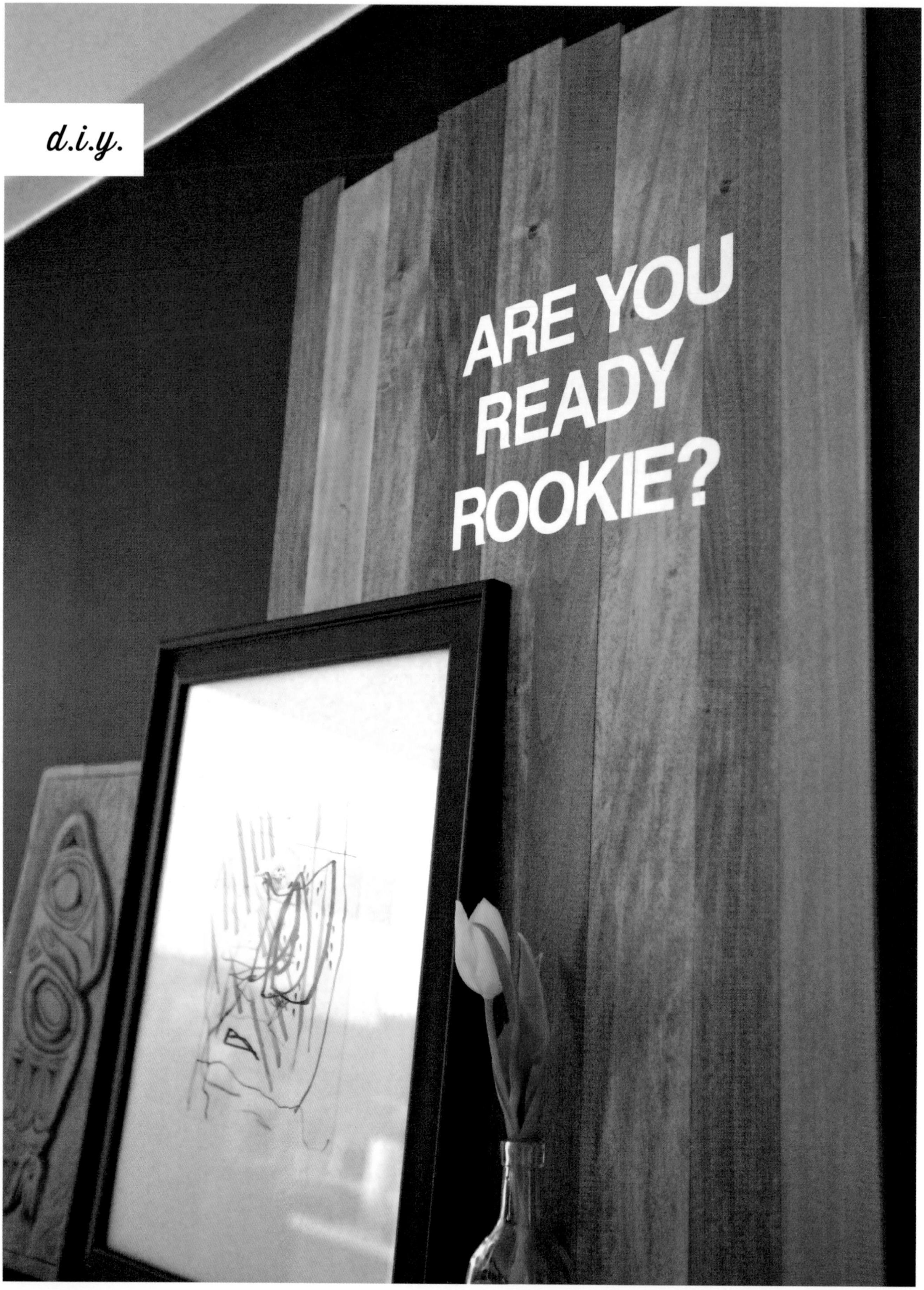

# QUOTABLE WALL ART

Here's an easy idea for creating wall art that incorporates a favorite quote or phrase. It could be a quote that inspires you, makes you laugh, or is an inside joke between you and your loved ones.

**SUPPLIES**

wood

wood stain

clean rags

wood glue

paint or letter stickers

*1.* Purchase or cut a few (8 to 10) long pieces of thin wood. Ours were varying sizes between 2½ and 3 feet tall.

*2.* Stain the wood a few slightly different tones. Optional: add a coat of polyurethane.

*3.* Use two pieces of wood and wood glue to adhere all the pieces together.

*4.* Add your quote to the front of the piece with paint or letter stickers. Another fun option might be to paint over the stickers and after they dry peel them away to create a relief.

# FOCUS ON DETAILS

It's important to choose the perfect couch or statement piece, but don't forget about the little details that make a house a home. Add a few special objects to an uncluttered bookshelf or coffee table. Frame and hang a cute drawing from your niece in a gallery wall with the rest of your art collection (where it belongs!). And for a special night of entertaining, add a few small vases of fresh flowers to give your living room life.

d.i.y.

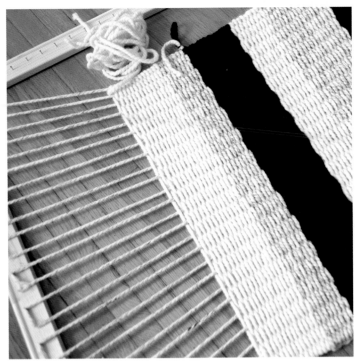

# YARN THROW PILLOWS

Can't find throw pillows that suit your color scheme? Try making your own! Here is a simple technique for creating your own loom and weaving your way to custom pillows.

### SUPPLIES

large wooden picture frame

nails

3 skeins of yarn (different colors if you like)

medium-thick interfacing

fabric (for the backs)

thread

Poly-fil

**1.** Create a loom by hammering nails along the top and bottom of the wooden frame.

**2.** String the yarn across all the nails and begin weaving your pattern, changing out colors as you go.

**3.** Once the front of the pillow is complete, iron on the interfacing to the backside of the woven yarn.

**4.** Stitch the woven yarn piece to a piece of fabric the same size, inside out, leaving a hole in one corner.

**5.** Flip through the hole and stuff with Poly-fil.

**6.** Sew up the hole and display your new pillow!

# CHOOSE YOUR COLOR SCHEME WITH CARE

Do you feel stressed over major furniture purchases? They feel like the biggest decision ever! When I was shopping for pieces for our new home, many people warned me that a neutral sofa was more practical. This bummed me out because I had my heart set on something colorful.

Here's what helped me: Before you make your first major furniture purchase, create a mood board and choose two or three fun colors to use throughout your rooms. Sticking with your favorite colors for major pieces is an easy way to create flow throughout the entire home. This solution is perfect for anyone obsessed with rearranging (cough, cough) because you can easily swap pieces from room to room! Choose your set of go-to colors that you love season after season and save the rest of the rainbow for accessories and accents.

d.i.y.

# HANGING PLANTS

Add life to your living room with these simple hanging vases made from recycled materials (you're welcome, Mother Earth).

**SUPPLIES**

3 tin cans (labels peeled off)

3 colors of spray paint

Crop-A-Dile (or hammer and nail)

twine or thin rope

scissors

*1.* Spray-paint the outside of each can with paint. Add a second coat of paint if needed and allow the paint to dry completely.

*2.* Use the Crop-A-Dile (or hammer and nail) to punch two holes across from each other near the top of the cans.

*3.* Cut a piece of twine 80 inches long and tie the middle 24 inches between the two holes of your top can to make a hanging handle.

*4.* Tie the twine through the middle can holes so that the bottom can hangs a foot lower than the top can.

*5.* Repeat step 4 with the lowest can and trim the extra twine.

*6.* Place a potted plant inside the can. You want the plant to remain in its plastic pot so that it has drainage but the outside (colorful) cans won't leak onto your living room floor.

# DESIGN FOR *YOUR* LIFESTYLE

Every room in your home should be designed for your lifestyle! If you notice a space that is rarely being used, reimagine its function. What do you use your living room for? Parties and game nights? Watching TV and movies after a long day? Hanging out with your dogs? Whatever your favorite activities, design your room to be a comfortable and welcoming space to do just that.

# FURNITURE FROM FOUND OBJECTS

Maybe you're living on a tight budget or maybe you love the thrill of a good flea market hunt! In either case, found objects can make incredible furniture. Make a pretty side table by stacking vintage file cabinets. Repurpose an old ladder by adding shelves and a fresh coat of paint for an adorable bookshelf! Search for interesting industrial pieces, like the vintage retail shelf on the opposite page, to hold plants and books you want to display.

BEFORE

AFTER

# RESTYLED COFFEE TABLE

Update an old, scuffed-up coffee table for your living room. A little paint and pattern can go a long way!

**SUPPLIES**

coffee table

sandpaper

tack cloth

balsa wood

wood glue

primer

white gloss latex paint

scissors

black electrical tape

**1.** Lightly sand the coffee table and wipe off any dust.

**2.** We wanted to cover the sides of this old coffee table. To do this, we measured the unwanted areas and used scissors to cut balsa wood to fit over the existing design.

**3.** Prime the coffee table with a primer. Once dry, paint 2 to 3 coats of white gloss latex paint, allowing drying time in between each coat.

**4.** Use scissors to cut 2-inch-long pieces of electrical tape and lay the pieces next to each other at different heights to create a zigzag pattern.

d.i.y.

# MAKE A STATEMENT WALL

Here is a bold way to add your favorite colors, patterns, or design to any space. A statement wall is a big commitment, so be sure to take time to plan out your design, but don't be afraid to go for it! Big changes are always a tiny bit scary.

**SUPPLIES**

thick card stock (for stencil)

scissors

painter's tape

oil pastels

clear spray sealer

small paintbrush

clear (water-based) polyurethane*

**1.** Create a custom stencil by cutting a design from the thick card stock. Make several of the same stencils if you want to do multiple tracings at once.

**2.** Tape your stencils to the wall and use the oil pastels to trace your outline.

**3.** Once your whole wall is stenciled, use a few coats of clear spray sealer to help seal your design.

**4.** Once the sealer is dry, use the small paintbrush to trace over each oil pastel stencil with the clear poly-urethane to help seal the oil pastel.

*Do not use oil-based polyurethane for this project as it can change the color of your wall paint.*

CELEBRATE

BIRTHDAY
COCKTAIL
PARTY

# BIRTHDAY CAKE MARTINI

MAKES 1

3 ounces marshmallow vodka
1 ounce cream of coconut
2 ounces amaretto
3 ounces Godiva white chocolate liqueur
Sprinkles for the rim

In a martini shaker combine the marshmallow vodka, cream of coconut, amaretto, and Godiva white chocolate liqueur. Add ice and shake.

Serve in a glass rimmed with sprinkles.

Once you've created a living space that you love, why not host a birthday cocktail party? As if we even need an excuse to invite friends over for a drink. Ha! Have fun with decorating your space, planning a few things to snack on, and mixing up a specialty birthday cocktail!

FILL YOUR CEILING WITH MULTI-COLORED BALLOONS! IF YOU HAVE A SMALL LIVING ROOM OR APARTMENT, THIS CAN BE QUITE AFFORDABLE.

CUT OUT SHAPES (LIKE A HEART) FROM POSTER BOARD AND FILL WITH TISSUE PAPER FRINGE TO HANG ON THE WALL.

YOU CAN ALSO FILL THE FLOOR WITH COLORFUL BALLOONS. NO HELIUM NEEDED!

# FLOWER VASES 9 WAYS

**1.**
COVER A GLASS VASE IN PATTERNED FABRIC AND SEAL WITH MOD PODGE.

**5.**
GLUE COLORED LEATHER TO THE OUTSIDE.

**6.**
COIL THIN ROPE OR RIBBON AROUND THE OUTSIDE OF A VASE.

**2.**
PAINT THE ENTIRE VASE WHITE AND THEN ADD DOODLES WITH A SHARPIE.

**3.**
COVER IN GLITTER! COME ON, YOU KNOW YOU WANT TO.

**4.**
PAINT WITH YOUR FAVORITE METALLIC TONE AND ADD POLKA DOTS.

**7.**
USE NATURAL FABRICS OR TWINE TO COVER YOUR FAVORITE VASE.

**8.**
CHALKBOARD PAINT! YOU KNOW WE HAD TO.

**9.**
PAINT ON YOUR FAVORITE QUOTE OR SONG LYRIC IN YOUR HANDWRITING.

# KITCHENS

*A kitchen needs to be* an inspiring space. It doesn't have to be large, or expensive, or perfect, but it absolutely *must* inspire. A beautiful kitchen makes cooking a treat, even if you're making a pot of ramen.

The kitchen is our favorite room to make over. It's crazy what a difference a little paint and some fresh flowers can do. In this chapter you'll see how we made over our dated, dark-wood kitchens and gave them a fresh dose of color!

Want to know a nerdy secret? We're also passionate about organizing our kitchens. Reorganizing cabinets and making new space for hard-to-store items is such a rewarding way to spend an afternoon. We geek out over cleaning, purging, and coming up with new solutions to store stuff. A cozy kitchen is a mix of both practical and eye-pleasing solutions. Now, let's get to it!

# CHOOSE A STATEMENT PIECE

Consider adding a statement piece that reflects your personality to spice up your neutral kitchen! You can go bold with vibrant artwork, colorful tile, or a vintage-inspired appliance. Our retro-style refrigerator was a gift from my husband when we moved into our home. It makes me smile every day and is a great conversation piece when guests visit for the first time.

## UPDATE YOUR OLD REFRIGERATOR

If a fancy new fridge doesn't fit your budget this year, no biggie! Try updating your existing fridge with electrical tape. The tape can easily be removed (in case your lease is up!) and is super easy to wipe down and clean.

**SUPPLIES**

white electrical tape

scissors

**1.** Sketch out your pattern on a piece of paper. We created a design based on Turkish kilim rugs.

**2.** Starting with the designs on the top and bottom, begin to cut your tape strips and apply the tape to the fridge.

**3.** For a cleaner look, cover any areas that have tape ends with a finishing piece of tape.

# GET ORGANIZED

Who doesn't love an organized kitchen? Even in the smallest space you can make room for the things you need to keep on hand by adding shelving, baskets, and labels! These locker baskets were an inexpensive find (from Amazon.com) and they are the perfect way to optimize the space above cabinets. Labeling a set of drawers is a fun way to keep spices and snacks where they belong. Have a free wall? Consider adding open shelving for constantly used items like glasses, pitchers, or a French press.

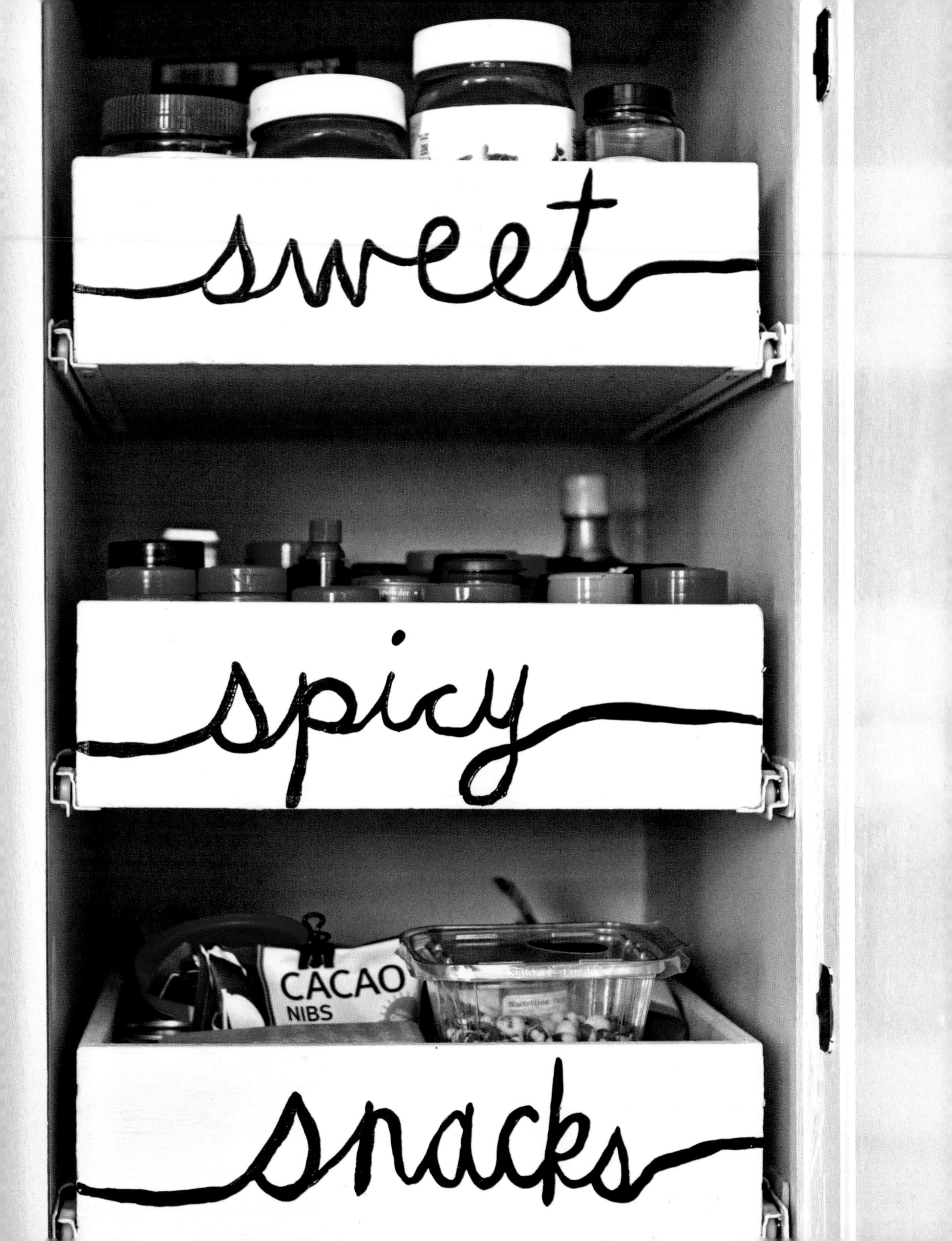
sweet
spicy
CACAO
NIBS
snacks

# KITCHEN RUG

Add some extra color to your kitchen floors with a bright hand-painted rug. You can use any colors or patterns that suit your kitchen aesthetic.

**SUPPLIES**

plain kitchen rug

ruler

marker

fabric paint

paintbrush

aerosol polycrylic protective finish (water based)

**1.** Use the ruler and marker to create a grid on one side of the rug.

**2.** Fill in each grid square using fabric paint with multiple colors/patterns of your choosing, covering over the marker lines.

**3.** Once the paint is fully dry, spray the rug with the protective finish. Make sure to read the instructions on your fabric paint brand—some require heat to set permanently.

# MODERNIZE YOUR CABINETS

If your kitchen is filled with dark wood cabinets that just don't suit your modern tastes, update them! Try giving them a fresh coat of paint in contrasting colors. Or you could change out your cabinet hardware; you'd be surprised how much this can transform the look of your space.

# COLORFUL ACCENT ART

It can be a challenge to add artwork to your kitchen walls. Most of your space may be taken up by cabinets, shelves, or other storage solutions. Create a colorful word or short phrase to add a bit of whimsy to your kitchen walls. You can use found wood to cut your own design or buy pre-made letters from a craft store.

### SUPPLIES

scrap paper

pencil

scissors

old wood pieces

saw

scrap wood

wood glue

paint

picture hanger hardware

**1.** Use scrap paper to create letters the size and shape that suit your space. Tape the letters to the wall you plan to hang them on, to make sure.

**2.** Use the paper as a pattern to cut the letters out of your wood pieces.

**3.** Use scrap wood and wood glue to glue the pieces together.

**4.** Paint the letters.

**5.** Add the picture frame hardware to the back of each letter and hang on your wall.

# CREATE A SPECIALTY CART

We don't always have the luxury to prepare a four-course meal every time we are in the kitchen. Often we simply want to make a quick cup of coffee or mix a cocktail for a friend. If you find you have specific needs that arise over and over again, try buying a metal cart (from a flea market or thrift store) and customizing it to suit your space. Make your own bar cart by assembling your favorite liquors and mixers. Or create a coffee cart so you have a spot to store your coffee beans, grinder, coffee maker, and all the accessories you need to make a great cup of joe.

# PERSONALIZED APRONS (2 WAYS)

Whether you plan to give these to your mom or keep one for yourself, personalizing an apron is such a simple and relaxing project! Here are two ideas to get your own creative juices flowing.

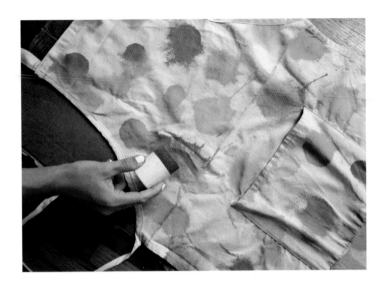

**SUPPLIES FOR ABSTRACT APRON**

plain canvas or cotton apron

spray bottle of water

fabric or acrylic paint

3 sizes of circle sponges

*1.* Spray water on the apron.

*2.* Water down the paint a little and use the sponges to stamp different-sized circles on your apron.

*3.* Before the paint dries, use the water bottle to spray each dot and diffuse the painted circles.

*4.* Continue with each color until the entire apron is covered.

**SUPPLIES FOR ILLUSTRATED APRON**

plain canvas or cotton apron

pencil

permanent marker

*1.* Use a pencil to outline your illustrations on the apron. Be sure you are completely happy with the placement.

*2.* Trace over your pencil lines using the paint marker. Allow to fully dry before use.

# DREAM HOUSE RECIPE BOX

Create a special recipe box for your kitchen or as a housewarming gift for a friend. Customize this project to match your dream (or actual) home!

**SUPPLIES**

construction paper

scissors

glue

cardboard house box (found at many craft stores; ours is from Hobby Lobby)

glue

Mod Podge (optional)

**1.** Cut out construction paper to be the siding, shingles, windows, and other features of the house.

**2.** Glue paper to the box with a thin coat so it doesn't bleed through.

**3.** If you would like to seal your recipe box, apply a coat of Mod Podge to the outside.

**4.** Fill the box with recipe cards and dividers and start filling it with your favorite dishes!

CELEBRATE

COOKIE
DECORATING
PARTY

KEEP IT SIMPLE. YOU DON'T NEED TONS OF DECORATIONS TO HAVE A GOOD TIME WITH YOUR GRANDMA.

FOCUS ON WHAT'S IMPORTANT—SPENDING TIME TOGETHER.

You might not think to throw a party in your kitchen. Most kitchens are filled with just a little too much chaos, right? Cooking tends to be messy, cluttered, sometimes fast paced, or even a little smoky. But often a little organized chaos can lead to some very special memories. Why not invite a few family members over to bake and decorate cookies? This is a special activity during the holidays, but it can become a tradition for any time of the year.

# OUR FAVORITE CHOCOLATE CHIP COOKIES

MAKES 2 DOZEN

*3½ cups all-purpose flour*
*1¼ teaspoons baking soda*
*1½ teaspoons baking powder*
*2 teaspoons salt*
*1¼ cups softened butter*
*1½ cups brown sugar*
*1 cup granulated sugar*
*2 eggs*
*1 teaspoon vanilla extract*
*2 cups dark or semisweet chocolate chips*

Preheat the oven to 350°F. In a bowl whisk together the flour, baking soda, baking powder, and salt. Set aside.

Cream together the softened butter and sugars. Add the eggs and vanilla extract and stir until just combined. Add the flour mixture to the creamed butter and mix until just incorporated. Stir in the chocolate chips until just combined.

Spoon the batter onto a baking sheet lined with parchment paper. Bake for 14 to 16 minutes, until the edges are just beginning to brown. Remove from the oven and move to a cooling rack. Serve warm with a glass of milk.

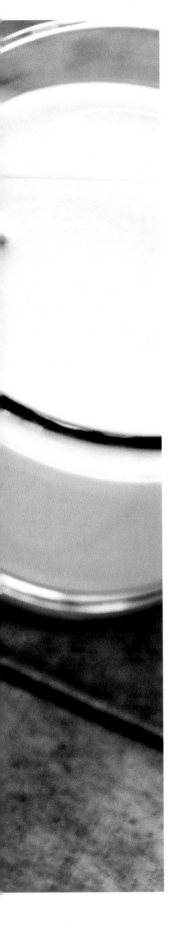

# COFFEE MUGS 9 WAYS

**TIP:** After using Sharpies on porcelain, simply bake the piece at 350°F for 30 minutes before use. For best results, always hand wash. If you are looking for a paint that is dishwasher safe, try Pebeo Porcelaine 150.

**1.**
ADD DOODLES WITH A SHARPIE.

**5.**
CREATE YOUR OWN "HIS" AND "HERS" MUGS WITH A LITTLE PAINT.

**6.**
COMPANION MUG.

**7.**
PUT YOUR HEART ON YOUR SLEEVE . . . OR, UH . . . MUG.

**2.**
METALLIC SHARPIE? OH YES.

**3.**
PAINT THE ENTIRE MUG WITH METALLIC PAINT, EXCEPT FOR THE RIM.

**4.**
DOODLE EDGES IN RED SHARPIE!

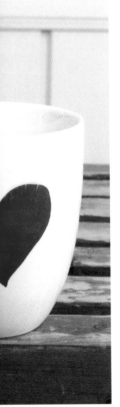

**8.**
ADD PERSONALITY WITH A LITTLE FACE ON THE FRONT OF YOUR MUG.

**9.**
ADD A PATTERN WITH SHARPIES.

# DINING

# ROOMS

———

*We love dining rooms* because they create the setting for one of everyone's favorite pastimes—eating. Don't even try to pretend you're not in this club. But when you really think about it, the dining room is a place where some of the most precious memories in your home are made. It is around the dining room table that we laugh with friends over cocktails, make big announcements over coffee with our parents, or share a laid-back but intimate breakfast with our significant other.

When we were in Palm Springs last spring I realized that the thing my dining room was missing was a restaurant vibe. I made lists of all the places I loved eating at and why. The results surprised me because the places I loved to be were very different from the rooms I liked in photos on Pinterest. Keeping with that theme, I finished designing my dining room with inspiration from all my favorite foodie spots and bars. The result was a cozier, happier dining room that is super versatile for parties year-round!

The best advice we can give for designing your dining room is to forget everything you think you know about what makes a nice dining room and create a place that's comfortable and exciting to eat in. Make meals a daily treat and a cherished ritual.

ooh you make me
live whatever this
world can give to
me it's you you're
all i see ooh you
make me live now
honey you're the
best friend that i
ever
with you
long

# MIX MODERN AND RUSTIC ELEMENTS

Mixing unexpected styles can add a lot of interest and energy to a room. This strategy is especially great if you are the kind of person who just can't commit to one particular style, or can't afford to change décor with every trend you love. You can't see it, but I'm raising my hand: guilty as charged. Try mixing a rustic wood table with modern plastic chairs. Combine a graphic rug with a classic chandelier. Whatever look you're going for, find a few small elements that might work together and combine them in one room.

## CUSTOM SERVING DISHES

Create your own custom serving dishes inspired by classic patterns, like Blue Willow china.

**SUPPLIES**

plain white dishes

blue Sharpie or ceramic pen

*1.* Draw on the surface of your dishes.

*2.* Bake for 30 minutes at 350°F.

*3.* Allow to cool completely before using or washing. To ensure that your designs last longer, try hand washing.

# HANGING GLASS VASES

If your dining room table is often too crowded to add fresh flowers, consider making a few hanging vases.

**SUPPLIES**

twine

duct tape

glass bud vases

**1.** Make a loop with the twine that is your desired hanging length for the vase.

**2.** Use the duct tape to secure this loop to the vase.

**3.** Run a piece of twine under the bottom of the vase and bring it up to the top.

**4.** Secure with tape, move the twine over a quarter turn, and loop down under the bottom of the vase again and back up again. Secure with tape.

**5.** Wrap the twine around the top of your vase to completely cover the duct tape and tie off to finish.

# BE CREATIVE

Shopping for dining room chairs is intimidating (and expensive!). Rather than biting the bullet on a new set, why not collect random chairs from flea markets and estate sales and give them a fresh coat of paint? Choose a color that really inspires you. This idea can save you more than a pretty penny, while creating a look that has personality and charm.

A painted piano can also serve a double purpose as an unexpected serving space. Layer it up with tiered cake stands and it's perfect for a quick impromptu dinner party with friends. I love a piece that can be used two ways, don't you?

# SIMPLE AND COLORFUL SIDE TABLE

Are you in need of additional serving space to host buffet-style dinners or to hold your growing liquor collection? Try making your own simple side table to match the colors of your dining room.

**SUPPLIES**

wooden sawhorse

wooden board for tabletop (36 by 20 inches)

paintbrushes

primer

white latex paint

orange latex paint

wood glue

**1.** First, prime your sawhorse and wooden board with primer.

**2.** Once the primer is dry, use the white paint to paint the top of your tabletop.

**3.** Paint the sawhorse with 2 to 3 coats of the orange (our color, but use your favorite).

**4.** With a smaller paintbrush, paint the side edge of your tabletop orange.

**5.** Add wood glue to the top of the sawhorse and center your board on top. Place a heavy object on top while the glue dries. If you plan to have lots of weight on this table, you should add screws to secure the two pieces together.

# CREATE A RESTAURANT VIBE

Defy tradition and get inspired for your dining room by your favorite cafés and coffee shops. Focus on happy vibes and cheerful times rather than matching furniture and décor.

In our space, we created a custom lighting fixture with a dimmer switch that creates a interesting atmosphere for daytime or evening hangouts. What else? Think bar carts, quirky buffet tables, comfortable seating, and interesting ways to serve appetizers—just to name a few! Bottom line: create a dining room that feels like your favorite restaurant and you'll find yourself inviting friends over much more often!

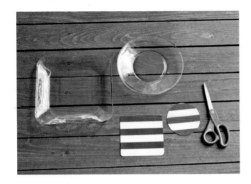

# MODERN CAKE STANDS

Here's an easy way to create cake stands to fit your own style. Use any patterned paper and paint color you like to make your cake stands unique.

**SUPPLIES**

patterned paper

scissors

glass plates and cups

Mod Podge

spray primer

spray paint

crazy glue

**1.** Cut patterned paper to fit the undersides of your plates. Use Mod Podge to glue in place and then seal.

**2.** Prime the cups.

**3.** Paint the cups once the primer is dry.

**4.** Glue the cups to the bottoms of the plates to create cake stands!

CELEBRATE

HOST A HAPPY
DINNER PARTY

# MENU

### ① Drinks
RASPBERRY MARGARITA
PEACH & BASIL MOJITO
ROSE WINE

### ② Dips
JALAPENO GUACAMOLE
HABANERO SALSA
MANGO SALSA

### ③ Dinner
CHIPOTLE SHRIMP TACOS
FETA & LIME CORN
CHIPOTLE MAYO

### ④ Dessert
SPICY HOT FUDGE SUNDAES

CREATE HANDMADE MENUS FOR EACH SETTING TO GREET GUESTS AS THEY ARRIVE.

**Décor Inspiration**

Don't stress yourself out with over-the-top decorations if you don't have the time or budget. Instead spend that money on a good bottle of wine for guests! If you do have the resources to add a few fancy touches, focus on table décor—most of the evening will be spent around the dining room table!

REUSE CLEAN COFFEE OR SOUP CANS AS VASES FOR COLORFUL FLOWERS . . .

. . . OR POKE HOLES IN THEM AND ADD TEA LIGHTS.

USE BANDANNAS AS CLOTH NAPKINS TO ADD A POP OF COLOR.

## What to Serve?

This is probably the most daunting question for a dinner party. A few things to consider before you dive into any recipe book or food blog: budget, your cooking skill level/comfort zone, and special dietary needs of guests. These three factors can really help you plan your menu.

- Go casual. Just because it's a dinner party doesn't mean it has to be fancy. You can totally host a taco and beer night.
- Be collaborative. A great way to keep a party budget friendly is to invite guests to join in preparing a dish. Have one couple bring the salad or a side dish while another guest brings dessert.
- Try classic dishes with a twist. Unexpected flavors can be fun and a great way to start conversations. Prepare a menu of gourmet comfort foods. Try vegan versions of your childhood favorite dishes. Choose a specific theme or ingredient and incorporate it into every course (lavender everything!).

# PEACH & BASIL MOJITO

MAKES 1

½ peach, cubed
Juice of ½ lime
4 basil leaves, chopped
4 mint leaves, chopped

2 ounces white rum
1 ounce simple syrup
Club soda

In a glass, combine the peach cubes, lime juice, basil, mint, rum, and simple syrup. Stir to combine. Add ice and top with club soda. Serve chilled.

# CLOTH NAPKINS 9 WAYS

**TIP:** Use fabric paint for best results. Read brand instructions, you may need to heat-set the paint to make it permanent!

## 1.
STAMP ON A FRUIT-INSPIRED PATTERN.

## 5.
USE FOAM LETTERS TO STAMP ON A QUOTE OR SONG LYRIC.

## 6.
SEW ON A MIX OF COLORFUL POLKA DOTS USING SCRAP FABRIC.

**2.**
PAINT ON AN ABSTRACT OR SIMPLIFIED FLORAL PATTERN.

**3.**
USE PERMANENT INK TO ADD A HAND-DRAWN PATTERN. SEW ON A DECORATIVE EDGE.

**4.**
PAINT ON A GRAPHIC DESIGN. BE BOLD!

**7.**
USE PERMANENT INK TO DRAW ON A NAUTICAL DESIGN. SEW ON A COLORFUL EDGE.

**8.**
USE FABRIC DYE TO CREATE A COLORFUL OMBRE PATTERN.

**9.**
USE COLORFUL THREAD TO STITCH ON A BORDER AND ADD TASSELS!

# BEDROOMS

***Bedrooms are an intimate affair.*** Your bedroom is your fortress of solitude. It should be designed for no one else but you and your significant other. This is a room that should feel VERY you. You aren't entertaining in this room. It's all you, baby!

Your bedroom should be where you want to wake up and where you can relax before falling asleep every night. It should feel familiar. It should be where you want to retreat after a long day. After all, the bedroom is where you do so many personal things, like get ready for a big day, read a favorite guilty pleasure book, or snuggle with your best friend.

Throughout this book we talk about finding ways to use your favorite colors or incorporate elements from your favorite hotel or restaurant. In your bedroom you can get even a little more personal. What colors or textures make you feel safe? What kind of music helps you wake up and get ready in the morning? Find ways to incorporate these feelings into the décor of your bedroom.

# TIPS FOR LIGHTING

Of all the rooms in a home, good lighting in the bedroom is most important. At night you want a room that is relaxed, private, and cozy. Lamps and diffused light sources are wonderful. A string of twinkle lights over a bed or strung around a vintage ladder can create the loveliest vibe.

In the daytime, you want the exact opposite! There's nothing lovelier than waking up to sunshine and beautiful natural light. Light airy curtains, like this lace set, are perfect for letting in gorgeous light. Design your room from day to night with both natural light and lamps that flatter your space and create a mood that makes you happy.

# COFFEE FILTER FLOWERS

Creating your own faux flowers from coffee filters is an easy and inexpensive way to add texture and a soft touch to any space. Try adding these flowers around the frame of a mirror, along the top of a window, or above your bed.

**SUPPLIES**

coffee filters

scissors

thumbtacks

*1.* For larger flowers, use two filters. For smaller flowers, fold two filters in half and cut off an inch of the filter from the top.

*2.* Wrinkle the filter and gently arrange into a flower shape.

*3.* Use thumbtacks to add flowers to any wood surface or dry wall.

# PATTERNED DUVET COVER

Here's a simple technique to create your own customized duvet and pillow covers. Add personality to your own bedroom or create a cute housewarming gift for a friend. (Newlywed gift? I think so!)

**SUPPLIES**

craft foam

scissors

cardboard

glue

fabric paint

white comforter and sham set

**1.** With scissors, cut the craft foam to create 9-inch-wide triangles and glue the foam onto cardboard squares to create a stamp. Make one for each color in your design.

**2.** Mix your fabric paint colors and apply a generous amount to your stamp.

**3.** Starting at the top corner of your comforter, press your stamp firmly onto your comforter and push down on each corner. Put some cardboard under the top layer of your comforter so the paint doesn't bleed through to the other side.

**4.** Repeat with each color, making rows across the top of the comforter, and continue until the whole area is completed.

**5.** Take your pillowcases and repeat the stamping process. Once everything is dry, you may need to iron the fabric so the paint is heat-set and permanent if you aren't using matte paint. Then you are ready for bedtime!

# THE WINDOW SEAT

There are endless possibilities for the window seat. If you've been lucky enough to find a space with one, it can be a place to read or a spot to store a collection or display beautiful things. I love it best when it's a little bit of both! Add a beautiful plant, a good book, a soft blanket, and personal elements like a guitar and some pillows. Now it's the perfect space to cozy up and relax!

# POPS OF
# COLOR + TEXTURE

Bedrooms shouldn't be boring! Don't be afraid to fill your space with color and texture if that's what makes you happy. Add a statement wall like this hand-painted wall behind our bed, a textured comforter, a fun natural rug, or a large piece of bold art.

# PAINTED DRESSER

Furniture can be such a commitment, right? You might not have the budget to buy that perfect piece you've been dreaming of (yet). You may have a few hand-me-down or thrift-store-bought items in your home that just don't quite feel like you. A great option is to give them a facelift with a fresh coat of paint! You could choose to cover the entire surface, just the faces of the drawers, or just the legs of a chair or table, or add a pattern by masking off areas with painter's tape. Use colors you love to spruce up a piece of furniture you aren't totally happy with.

*1.* Clean all surfaces you plan to paint first.

*2.* Lightly sand the surface, which allows the paint to adhere better.

*3.* Always prime first. This will really make your color choices stand out.

*4.* Don't stress yourself out about the perfect color. Feel free to experiment and explore; you can always repaint next month if you end up hating it. No big deal!

## FAMILY PHOTO BOOTH DISPLAY

Not sure what to do with those cute photo booth pictures? The shape can be a little challenging to work with, but try cutting balsa wood to fit your frame and photo to display on your walls.

# SCENTED CANDLES

Create your own quirky candles with your favorite scents. These are super cute to add to your bedside table or to give to a friend. You can use any glass or ceramic objects that you like, so keep your eyes peeled on your next flea market shopping trip.

## SUPPLIES

glass or ceramic objects

plain candle wax (can be found at most craft stores)

essential oils

wicks

wax paper

paint

**1.** Clean your candle vessels.

**2.** Melt the wax according to the brand's instructions. Add in your essential oils for scent. Pour into the vessels.

**3.** Add the wicks. To keep them centered, place a sheet of wax paper over the vessel with a small hole in the middle for the wick to poke through.

**4.** Once the candle has fully set, remove the wax paper. Add a little paint to the outside of your objects for color.

# KEEP SCALE IN MIND

You don't want your room to feel too full, making you feel boxed in. You also don't want your space to feel too unintentionally bare. I'm all for minimalism, but your space shouldn't feel like you're still moving in and haven't had time to set everything up yet. Note the size and scale of your room. If you have high ceilings, you might consider adding elements that draw the eye up, filing the space. This could include an oversized bedframe, hanging lanterns, a large tapestry, or a gallery wall that fills up the space. If your bedroom is on the cozy side, avoid large pieces of furniture or low-hanging light fixtures.

*d.i.y.*

# WALL ART (2 EASY WAYS)

You don't have to be a professional painter or illustrator to create something special for your bedroom walls. Don't be afraid to try your hand at making your own artwork! Here are two simple ideas to get you started.

**SUPPLIES**

copy paper

watercolor paints

paintbrushes

white canvas

acrylic or craft paint

Sharpie pens or markers

*1.* To get the look above, print off a black-and-white photo you've taken onto regular (copy) paper. Choose a few colors you love and paint a thin coat of color over the picture. You could use watercolor paints or acrylic paints diluted with water.

*2.* For the painting on the opposite page, get a plain white canvas plus a few acrylic or craft paints in your favorite colors. Paint on a few layers of one design (like messy flowers), allowing each layer to dry in between coats. Use different color Sharpie pens or markers to add messy borders to your designs.

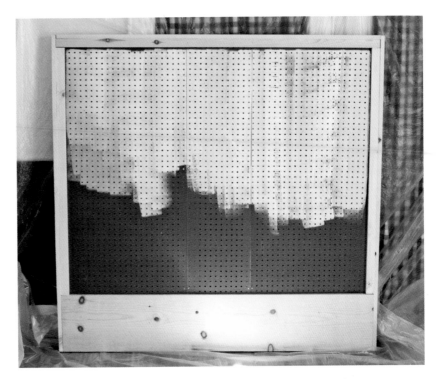

# GUEST ROOM BED FRAME

Welcome guests with magazines, snacks, or extra toiletries hung on this simple pegboard bed frame. You can customize this project to fit your guest room's bed size.

**SUPPLIES**

enough pegboard to cover 50 by 60 inches (we used three pieces measuring 12 by 50 inches, 24 by 50 inches, and 24 by 50 inches)

1 (12-by-1½-by-60-inch) wood piece (we used all pine)

2 (2-by-2-by-60-inch) wood pieces

3 (1-by-1½-by-60-inch) wood pieces (we used all pine)

2 (1-by-1½-by-48-inch) wood pieces

screws

screwdriver

drill

primer and colorful paint (optional)

paintbrushes (optional)

wood accent

pegboard hooks

*1.* Secure the pegboard to the 12-by-1½-by-60-inch wood piece with the 2 (2-by-2-by-60-inch) pieces in the back (see images).

*2.* Create a frame around your pegboard front with the 3 (1-by-1½-by-60-inch) and 2 (1-by-1½-by-48-inch) wood pieces.

*3.* Prime the entire front and sides of the bed frame, if desired.

*4.* Add an accent, like a little black heart, to the front.

*5.* Add your pegboard hooks and hang items for guests.

## JEWELRY DISH 9 WAYS

**TIP:** We like using Mod Podge to seal our designs in place after they've dried, no matter if they are created with paper, paint, or colorful pens.

**1.**
GLUE FABRIC OR RIBBON TO THE UNDERSIDE OF A GLASS PLATE.

**5.**
GET YOUR GLITTER ON! GLUE A THICK LAYER OF GLITTER AND SEAL WITH EPOXY.

**6.**
CREATE A COLLAGE FROM FOUND PAPERS AND GLUE TO THE UNDERSIDE OF A GLASS DISH.

**2.**

HI THERE, FUNNY FACE. PAINT A LAYERED DESIGN ON THE UNDERSIDE OF A GLASS PLATE.

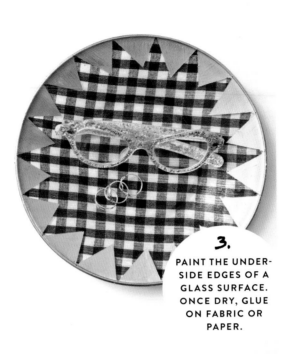

**3.**

PAINT THE UNDER-SIDE EDGES OF A GLASS SURFACE. ONCE DRY, GLUE ON FABRIC OR PAPER.

**4.**

ADD A VIBRANT COLOR WHEEL DESIGN!

**8.**

GLUE A PRETTY FLORAL PATTERNED FABRIC TO THE UNDERSIDE OF YOUR PLATE.

**7.**

TRY PAINTING ON A BLOCK DESIGN. USE MASKING OR PAINTER'S TAPE TO KEEP LINES STRAIGHT.

**9.**

PAINT ON A QUOTE OR FAVORITE SONG LYRIC!

# STUDIO
# SPACES

—

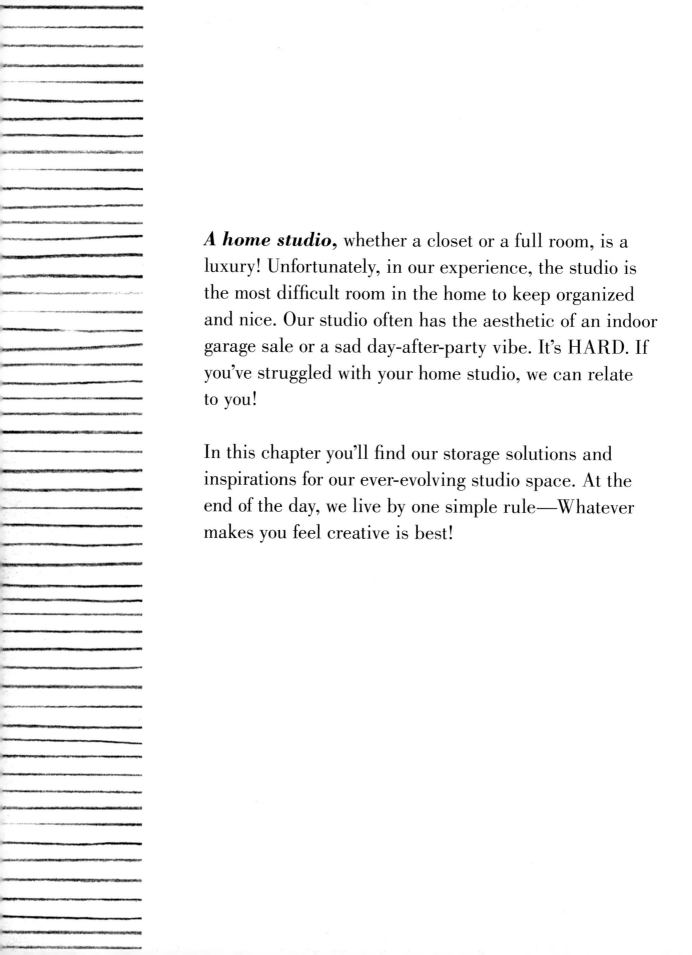

*A home studio,* whether a closet or a full room, is a luxury! Unfortunately, in our experience, the studio is the most difficult room in the home to keep organized and nice. Our studio often has the aesthetic of an indoor garage sale or a sad day-after-party vibe. It's HARD. If you've struggled with your home studio, we can relate to you!

In this chapter you'll find our storage solutions and inspirations for our ever-evolving studio space. At the end of the day, we live by one simple rule—Whatever makes you feel creative is best!

# FIND THE PERFECT PLACE

Most rooms in a house are already designated spaces. You don't really get to choose where the kitchen goes. But a studio or home office is a different story. First consider if you can dedicate an entire room to your studio. Do you have an extra guest bedroom or a finished basement or attic room? And if you can justify the space, consider converting a closet into an office or installing a fold-out table in a cabinet or wardrobe that could become your crafting corner. Find a space, no matter the size, that can be all yours.

d.i.y.

# MAKE OVER A FLOOR LAMP

Add some color and personality to your favorite floor lamp.

**SUPPLIES**

plain white lampshade

object for stamping
(we used a wine cork)

fabric paints

paintbrushes

*1.* Use a clean wine cork or other recycled object as your stamp.

*2.* Apply paint and stamp away! Use fabric paint and check your bottle for dry times. If your stamp looks too irregular, you can touch up any spots using a paintbrush.

*3.* Use a different, contrasting color to paint the trim or rim of the lampshade.

# CREATE
# A HAPPY
# WORKSPACE

Your studio space should, above all, make you feel happy. Decide what elements need to be present for you to feel inspired and motivated to work. Move your studio to an area in your home with a lot of sunlight if this helps you create. Add candles or cozy touches to your space that will stimulate all your senses and make you feel excited to make something in this space.

# STASH YOUR SUPPLIES

Studios of all different sizes often face a similar challenge—storage. You don't want your space to feel too cluttered, so find ways to stash your supplies to keep your space tidy. You could add a wall of labeled storage boxes to your craft room, or install a pegboard to hang tools or utensils. Use filing cabinets as the legs to your desk or stack a few vintage suitcases into a side table. Make these items work double duty as a storage solution and a piece of furniture.

d.i.y.

# UPDATE A FLEA MARKET CHAIR

The perfect office chair can be so hard to find! You may need a chair for your desk or sewing station, or to decorate a corner (like a mini bookshelf). Whatever your needs, consider updating an old chair to add personality to your space.

**SUPPLIES**

metal chair with plastic seat

gold spray paint for metal

white gloss spray paint for plastic

scissors

card stock

pencil

small paintbrush

gold craft paint

**7.** Use the gold spray paint to paint the legs of your chair (you can cover the seat with plastic first, or you can check to see if the legs will detach from the seat).

**2.** Use the white spray paint to paint the seat of your chair.

**3.** Using scissors and card stock, make a small star stencil and trace your stars with a pencil onto the surface of the chair (seat and back).

**4.** Using a small brush and gold craft paint, fill in your stars until your design is complete.

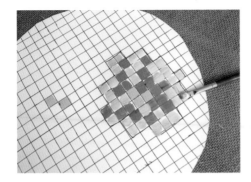

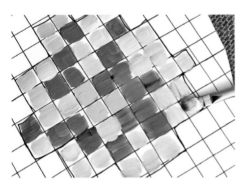

# CROSS-STITCH STOOL

Revamp a studio stool with this easy reupholstering technique.

**SUPPLIES**

graph paper

colored pencils

craft paint

½ yard burlap fabric

yarn

needle

scissors

staple gun

**1.** Create a grid template on graph paper of your own design (we did flowers). Use paint to copy the squares of color onto ½ yard of burlap.

**2.** Once the paint is dry, cover the squares with the same color yarn, cross-stitching as you go.

**3.** Use a staple gun to attach the burlap to your stool.

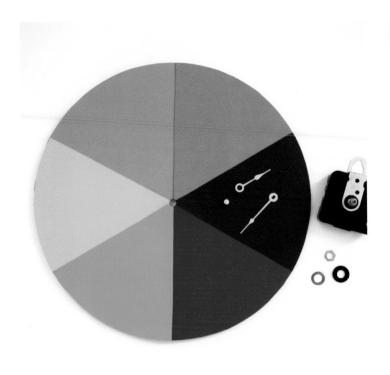

# COLOR WHEEL CLOCK

No office is complete without a clock, right? Make a colorful statement with this functional item.

**SUPPLIES**

foam board

X-Acto knife

6 colors of paper

ruler

pencil

scissors

glue

clock kit (available at most craft stores)

white craft paint

chipboard number stickers

**1.** Cut an 11-inch circle out of foam board with an X-Acto knife.

**2.** Use the colored paper to cut out 6 triangles that are 5½ inches wide. Glue the paper onto the foam to create your color wheel.

**3.** Cut a hole in the middle of the circle with the X-Acto knife and assemble the clock kit per the instructions through the hole.

**4.** Use the white craft paint to paint the clock hands and chipboard numbers and place the numbers in the correct positions.

# SUPPLY BASKETS 9 WAYS

**TIP:** Fabric or acrylic paint works well on these baskets. Feel free to use a heavy hand with the paint, as these won't get washed so there's less chance the paint will chip or crack.

**1.**

PAINT ON A POLKA DOT DESIGN.

**5.**

PAINT THE BOTTOM HALF OF THE BASKET FOR A FUN POP OF COLOR.

**6.**

STITCH ON A NOVELTY PATTERN.

**2.**
USE MASKING OR PAINTER'S TAPE TO EASILY ADD A PAINTED STRIPE DESIGN.

**3.**
ON WOVEN BASKETS, USE A TAPESTRY NEEDLE TO ADD A COLORFUL YARN ACCENT.

**4.**
STITCH ON AN ABSTRACT HEART IN THE CENTER.

**7.**
USE YARN, PAINT, AND FABRIC TO ADD AN ANIMAL TO YOUR BASKET.

**8.**
ADD SOME SUBTLE PERSONALITY WITH A LITTLE PAINT AND A FEW HOMEMADE TASSELS.

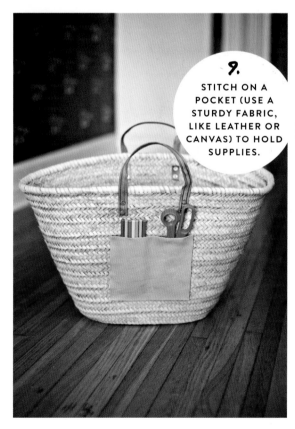

**9.**
STITCH ON A POCKET (USE A STURDY FABRIC, LIKE LEATHER OR CANVAS) TO HOLD SUPPLIES.

# OUTDOOR
# SPACES

———

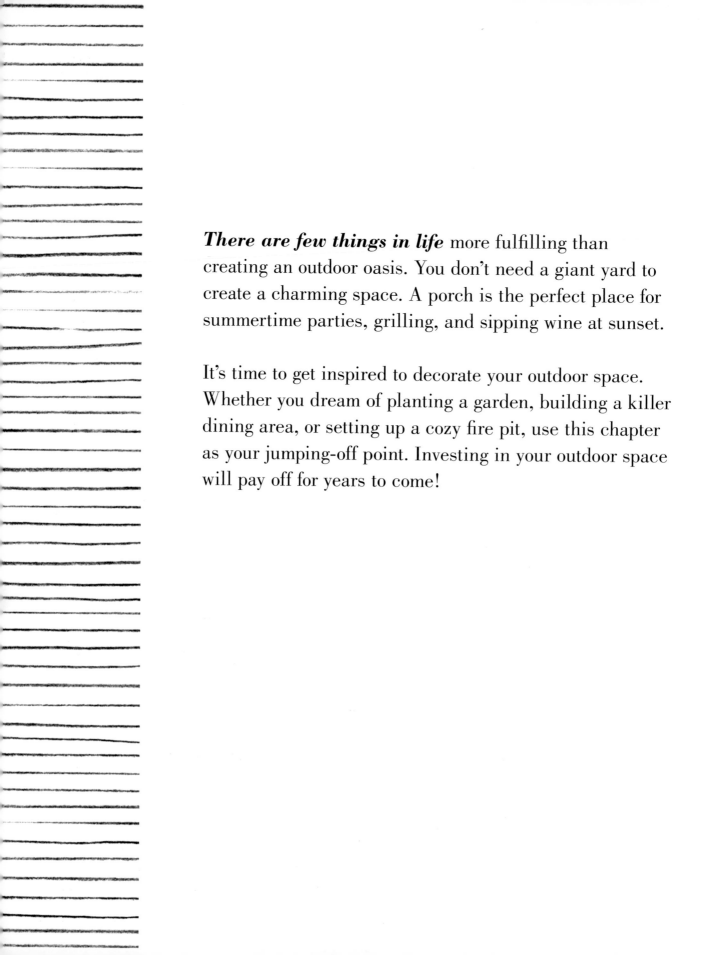

**There are few things in life** more fulfilling than creating an outdoor oasis. You don't need a giant yard to create a charming space. A porch is the perfect place for summertime parties, grilling, and sipping wine at sunset.

It's time to get inspired to decorate your outdoor space. Whether you dream of planting a garden, building a killer dining area, or setting up a cozy fire pit, use this chapter as your jumping-off point. Investing in your outdoor space will pay off for years to come!

## MOOD LIGHTING

Lighting is one of the most important choices you'll make when designing your outdoor space. Add outdoor string lights, lights in trees, and candles to create an inviting area. Don't be afraid to mix options, because in the backyard the more lighting, the merrier.

# OUTDOOR LANTERNS

Add a warm glow to your next outdoor get-together with these personalized lanterns. You can add any color or pattern you prefer!

**SUPPLIES**

black kerosene lanterns

paper straws

white craft paint

Q-tips

small paintbrush

**1.** On your first lantern, dip the tip of a paper straw into a small amount of white craft paint and use the straw end as a stamp to make circles on your lamp surface. Repeat until the whole surface is covered.

**2.** For the second lantern, dip a Q-tip into the paint and use the tip to make a dotted pattern. Repeat until the whole surface is covered.

**3.** For the third lantern, use a small paintbrush to brush the craft paint in small strokes to create a line texture on your lantern. Repeat until the whole surface is covered.

# BOX GARDEN + PATH

When we were growing up, our parents always kept a large garden, but for whatever reason we were always a little intimidated to grow our own. Instead of starting with a gigantic garden, why not try a simple raised box garden? We started with a short list of vegetables and herbs. Box gardens are cool because they can easily be expanded in years to come as your interest (and, ahem, skill level) grows. Be sure to use untreated cedar for your box; you don't want any chemicals in your food!

# HERB GARDEN

Are you dreaming of having a garden one day but your "backyard" is currently nothing more than a fire escape? Don't let this tiny detail stop you. A great way to work with limited space is to start a potted herb garden. And if you like cooking at home, you'll love having your own fresh herbs within reach!

**SUPPLIES**

ceramic pots

craft paint

brushes

Sharpie marker

potting soil

rocks and herb plants (start from seeds or buy plants and keep them going all season)

*1.* Try painting a few terracotta pots to match your aesthetic (don't paint the interiors).

*2.* Place a small rock over the hole in the bottom of the pot before filling it with soil. This allows the water to better soak into the soil before the excess drains out the bottom.

*3.* If you've never grown herbs (or any plants) before, don't feel like you have to start from seeds. You can buy most herbs (as well as vegetables and flowers) already sprouted and work to keep them alive and thriving.

# WORK WITH EXISTING FEATURES

What do you do if your budget just won't allow for you to build on a new deck or install fancy outdoor lights? You might feel a little lost on how you can make your outdoor space feel like you without breaking the bank. Your best bet is to work with existing features. Maybe you can't repaint your siding, but what about painting the back door? Can't splurge on matching outdoor furniture? Try using old, mismatched chairs (if you don't have some, you could thrift some) and giving them new life with outdoor paint and weather-friendly fabric like oilcloth. Show off your personality through the colors and patterns you add to existing elements in your space and have fun with it!

# SETTING UP FOR ENTERTAINING

Don't forget to add elements to your outdoor space with entertaining in mind. Add a cozy hammock or outdoor seating that will get people active or encourage conversation.

# RESTYLED OUTDOOR TABLE

Reimagine an old piece of outdoor furniture and give it a new life.

**SUPPLIES**

wooden or metal outdoor furniture piece

brushes

primer

indoor/outdoor paint

polyurethane

*1.* Prime the surface of your furniture. Allow to fully dry.

*2.* Paint over the primer with your paint choices. Allow to fully dry.

*3.* Seal with a layer of polyurethane for extra protection from outdoor elements.

**TIPS:**

• If your surface is super smooth, try roughing it up with heavy-duty sandpaper before priming. This can help paint to stick to the surface better.

• Always check paint and sealer cans for dry time suggestions.

• If you are not painting the entire surface, tape off the areas with painter's tape before you begin.

• Give yourself permission to get creative with your color choices! No matter how well we try to protect our outdoor furniture, it's not going to last forever, so have fun with it.

*Note: Polyurethane can slightly change the color of the paint it seals, especially whites.*

## COLOR COORDINATING

One easy way to add continuity to your outdoor space is to focus on one statement color. We chose pumpkin and wse picked out orange chairs and an orange grill and painted our shed the same color. These details tie the space together, without feeling super matchy-matchy. Be sure to work in plenty of neutrals, like natural wood and stone, to complement your choice.

# PICNIC BLANKET

Make a picnic blanket to match your outdoor aesthetic. You can use this blanket at your next outdoor party or take it with you on a picnic lunch to the park with your partner.

### SUPPLIES

scissors

craft foam

glue

cardboard

small paintbrush

fabric paint

white cotton tablecloth

**1.** With scissors, cut out a pattern from the craft foam and glue your foam onto a cardboard backing to create your stamp.

**2.** Use the paintbrush to brush the fabric paint onto your stamp, then apply the stamp to the tablecloth.

**3.** Reapply paint to your stamp and continue the pattern until the tablecloth is fully covered. Allow to fully dry before use. Make sure to read the instructions on your fabric paint brand—some require heat to set permanently.

# CELEBRATE

LADIES'
BACKYARD
BRUNCH

THROW A GARDEN PARTY IN YOUR OUTDOOR SPACE (NO GARDEN REQUIRED!). HOST A PARTY FOR MOTHER'S DAY OR JUST TO GET YOUR FAVORITE FRIENDS TOGETHER ON THE WEEKEND. SERVE UP YOUR FAVORITE BREAKFAST FOODS AND DRINKS AND ENJOY THE MORNING TOGETHER.

**Décor Inspiration**

Outdoor spaces often don't need as much added decoration, depending on the season. Add a few temporary touches to make your space feel cheerful.

USE TAPE (SUCH AS WASHI OR COLORFUL DUCT TAPE) TO ADD PATTERN TO AN OUTDOOR TABLE.

TISSUE PAPER FLOWERS AND STREAMERS ARE ALWAYS FESTIVE.

ADD A HOME-MADE BANNER OVER THE DRINK OR FOOD AREA.

# CINNAMON AND OLIVE OIL WAFFLES

**MAKES 6 TO 8 WAFFLES**

1½ cups flour
½ cup cornstarch
1 teaspoon baking soda
1 teaspoon salt
1 tablespoon brown sugar
½ teaspoon cinnamon
2 cups buttermilk
⅔ cup olive oil
2 eggs
1 teaspoon vanilla extract

In a large bowl, combine the flour, cornstarch, baking soda, salt, brown sugar, and cinnamon. Whisk. Stir in the buttermilk, olive oil, eggs and vanilla extract. Allow the batter to rest for 20 minutes. Follow waffle iron directions to cook the batter. Serve warm with lots of toppings: fresh berries, banana slices, chocolate chips, and sliced almonds. And don't forget the maple syrup!

## What to Serve?

Don't you just love breakfast foods!? You can keep the fare light and simple with a bagel and cream cheese spread. Or get more creative with a mix of sweet pastries, interesting flavored quiches, or a flight of bacon. Give guests options to mix flavors with their favorite breakfast breads, such as pancakes or waffles.

For drinks, consider setting up a mimosa or Bloody Mary bar. Provide the basics plus special ingredients to allow guests to create their own unique flavors. For example, if you are hosting a mimosa bar, be sure to have a few champagnes available and also a sparkling wine or prosecco. It's also a good idea to have a nonalcoholic option available when hosting a party. Let guests mix their own with a juice of their choice, such as orange, grapefruit, or blueberry. Top the drinks with fresh berries or fruit slices.

# TERRA-COTTA POTS 9 WAYS

**TIP**: Paint only the outside of the pots. The inside should remain unpainted in case you'd like to grow herbs or edible plants in your decorative pots.

**1.**

ADD A WHITE AND METALLIC POLKA DOT DESIGN IN PAINT.

**5.**

PAINT ON A FREEHAND GEOMETRIC DESIGN.

**6.**

GLUE ON FOAM PIECES AND THEN SPRAY-PAINT THE ENTIRE POT FOR A RAISED DESIGN.

**2.**

USE MASKING OR THIN PAINTER'S TAPE TO ADD A STRIPE DESIGN IN PAINT.

**3.**

PAINT ONLY THE BOTTOM HALF OF THE POT WITH A GRAPHIC EDGE.

**4.**

ADD A BOLD BLACK-AND-WHITE PATTERN.

**7.**

TRY ADDING COLORFUL POLKA DOTS!

**8.**

PAINT A RAINBOW OR COLORFUL STRIPES. DON'T BE AFRAID OF MESSY LINES!

**9.**

PAINT THE POT WHITE, THEN ADD A FAVORITE QUOTE OR SONG LYRICS IN SHARPIE.

# PLAYROOMS

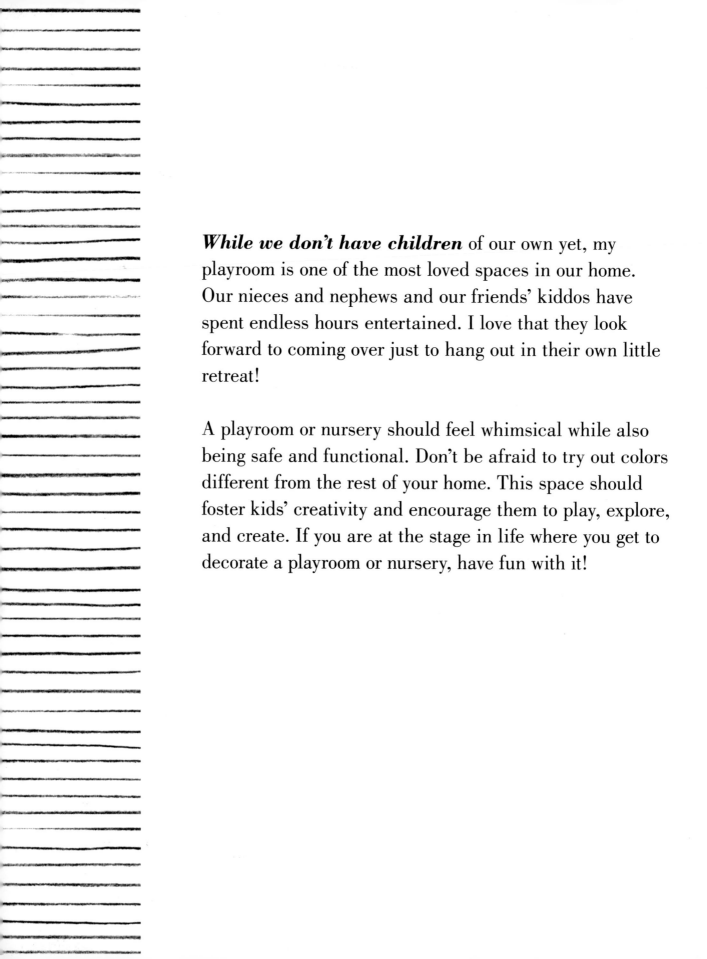

**While we don't have children** of our own yet, my playroom is one of the most loved spaces in our home. Our nieces and nephews and our friends' kiddos have spent endless hours entertained. I love that they look forward to coming over just to hang out in their own little retreat!

A playroom or nursery should feel whimsical while also being safe and functional. Don't be afraid to try out colors different from the rest of your home. This space should foster kids' creativity and encourage them to play, explore, and create. If you are at the stage in life where you get to decorate a playroom or nursery, have fun with it!

### SWING SEAT

A swing in the playroom is every kid's dream, and the best part is, it's totally doable! When choosing a spot for your swing, remember that you'll have to be flexible and work with the existing placement of the studs in your ceiling. We had our homemade swing professionally installed for safety. It's important that the swing is able to hold the weight of an adult. Choose a fun color to paint your swing base and go for it. You'll be glad you did!

## CONFETTI WALL

Playrooms are meant to be a fun place, so choosing a happy statement design for your wall only makes sense! Gather your painting supplies and choose a color that speaks happiness to you, like this confetti-inspired wall!

# PLUSH FARM ANIMALS

Turn your animal sketches into reality by creating your own plush farm animals. Simply sketch out a few patterns and bring them to life with cotton fabric, Poly-fil, and yarn. You could also buy a few plain plush animals and add your own embellishments, like a felt hair bow or multicolored yarn for a horse's mane.

### SUPPLIES

| | |
|---|---|
| scrap paper | needle |
| scissors | thread |
| fabric | Poly-fil |
| felt | fabric glue |
| yarn | |

*1.* Start by sketching out a few simple animal shapes. Create a pattern (from scrap paper) of the body of each animal (this should include the head, body, and feet). Cut out two pieces of fabric from this pattern that mirror each other.

*2.* Now add any other elements needed like tails, noses, yarn for the hair, and so on.

*3.* Stitch the body pieces together, leaving a small opening on one side. Flip inside out, then stuff with Poly-fil. Stitch up the hole.

*4.* Use fabric glue to add on the other elements.

d.i.y.

# KIDS' ART GALLERY WALL

If you have creative kids in your life, then your refrigerator, office drawers, or closet might be overflowing with beautiful art. Why not create a kids' art gallery wall in your playroom or nursery?

**SUPPLIES**

2 to 3 wooden boards the height of your desired gallery wall

screws

power drill

wire

staple gun

paint (optional)

wooden clothespins

**1.** Attach the boards to the wall in vertical lines. If your gallery wall is super large, you may want to have three rows of boards to break up the space.

**2.** Measure wire to fit across your boards (you could also use heavy-duty string). Add screws to the boards. String the wire (or heavy-duty string) across the screws, wrapping around each as you go.

**3.** Use a staple gun to further secure the wire in place.

**4.** Paint the boards and wire to match your walls, if you want the gallery wall to blend in. Grab some wooden clothespins and you're ready to start displaying all those beautiful creations.

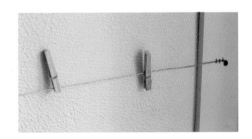

## PLAY SPACE

Create a play space that nurtures imagination! Choose toys with funny personalities; build your own A-frame tent and stock up on books and pillows to inspire hours of reading and storytelling!

*d.i.y.*

## WAGON BOOKSHELF

Need more space to house all that great kid literature you're collecting? Try updating a wooden wagon to be a mobile bookshelf.

**SUPPLIES**

Radio Flyer–style wagon

primer

white spray paint for wood/metal

card stock

teal and yellow craft paint

**1.** Remove the wooden sidepiece from one of the four wagon sides.

**2.** Use the primer to paint the rest of the wooden sides as well as the rubber wheels.

**3.** Use the white spray paint to paint the entire wagon white (we needed at least 2 to 3 coats of spray paint).

**4.** Once the paint is dry, use the card stock to make a triangle template and trace your triangles along the front and sides of the wagon. Use the teal craft paint to fill in the triangles. Paint the inside of the front wheels with the yellow craft paint.

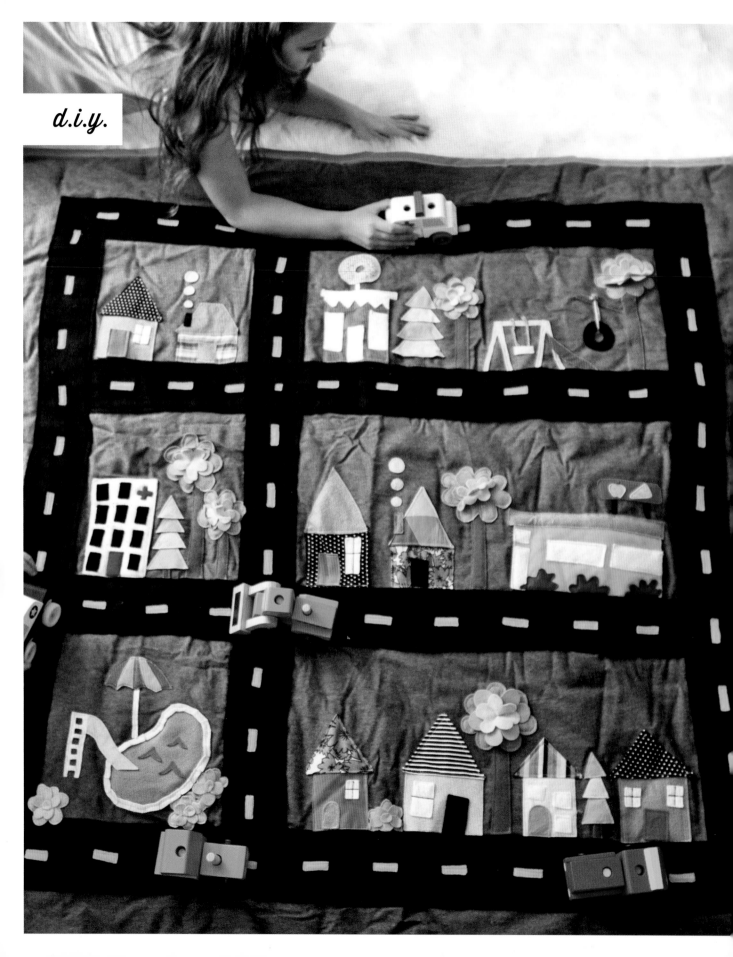

# PLAYTIME BLANKET

Create a mini city for kids to use with toy cars and figures in this playtime blanket project. No sewing required!

**SUPPLIES**

felt

scissors

fabric glue

plain thick blanket

*1.* From the felt, cut out shapes to create your mini city. Don't forget roadways, buildings, and trees.

*2.* Glue the shapes onto the blanket and allow to fully dry. Now you're ready to let the kids' imaginations run wild!

### RESTYLED ROCKING HORSE

Update an old or plain rocking horse to fit your aesthetic. If you get lucky you may be able to find a gently used (but maybe a little worn-looking) rocking horse at a flea market or thrift store. You can also usually find plain wood ones at most craft stores.

Ideas for updating your rocking horse:
• Paint the entire horse white; mask stripes off with tape and paint those black. Zebra!
• Get the kids involved and paint the horse multiple colors. Now that's a horse of many colors.
• Adhere a small wooden pyramid or short dowel rod. Now you have a unicorn!

CELEBRATE

KID'S BIRTHDAY
PARTY

FILL CLEAR BALLOONS WITH GLITTER OR PAPER CONFETTI.

MAKE YOUR OWN FESTIVE TABLECLOTH BY SIMPLY BUYING FABRIC IN A FUN PATTERN OR TEXTURE.

DECORATE PRESENTS WITH PLAIN WHITE PAPER AND RAINBOW-COLORED YARN OR HANDWRITTEN DOODLES.

## Décor Inspiration

Keep the party area clutter free so your little guests have plenty of space to play! Try keeping the presents and snacks condensed to one table/area. Focus your décor efforts in this spot; here are a few fun ideas:

KEEP THE FOCUS ON CELEBRATING TOGETHER RATHER THAN FUSSY DECORATIONS OR A PERFECTLY CLEAN HOME.

CREATE MEMORIES FOR YOUR LITTLE GUESTS WITH LITTLE SURPRISES, LIKE THESE CUPCAKE TOPPERS.

# CUPCAKE SURPRISE

Here's a fun activity that will have your little guests laughing with surprise. Cut a small hole in the center of each cupcake. Fill with a small plastic ball filled with different colored mini toys (like bouncy balls). Cover with frosting and let guests discover the surprise.

Mini toys work well with older children but can be hazardous for small children. If you are concerned the toys may be a choking hazard, use mini candy bars, jelly beans, or other edible/chewable options as the surprise instead. Guests will love comparing surprises with one another's.

# THROW PILLOWS 9 WAYS

**TIP:** When adding painted elements (for a no-sew project), be sure to use fabric paint and heat-set with an iron.

**1.**
ADD A COLORFUL PATCHWORK PATTERN.

**5.**
MASK OFF A MESSAGE (OR NUMBERS), THEN PAINT AROUND THAT AREA.

**6.**
STITCH ON A FELT DESIGN, LIKE TRIANGLES OR POLKA DOTS.

**2.**
ADD BOLD STRIPES AND STITCH ON A COLORFUL TRIM FOR THE BORDER.

**3.**
ADD A FUN MESSAGE OR QUOTE.

**4.**
STITCH A SQUARE (VINTAGE) SCARF TO THE FRONT OF A PILLOW.

**7.**
ADD PAINTED STRIPES, A SEW-ON FELT HEART, AND HOMEMADE TASSELS TO THE EDGES.

**8.**
STITCH ON RIBBON, TRIM, OR POM-POM TASSELS.

**9.**
STITCH ON DIFFERENT PIECES OF FABRIC TO ADD CONTRAST.

# SMALL
# SPACES

———

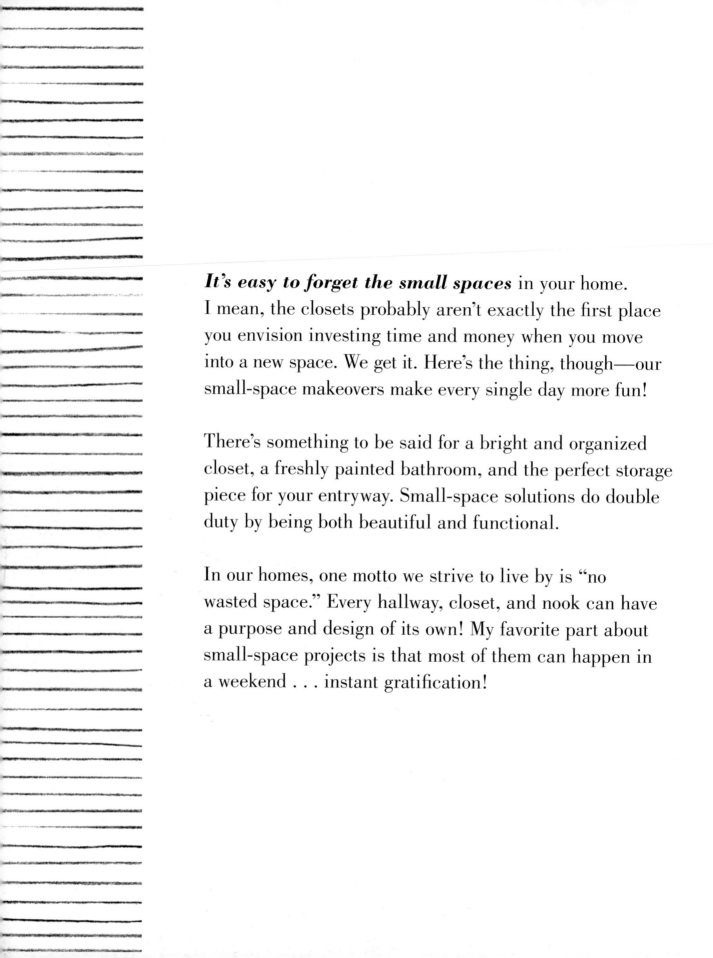

***It's easy to forget the small spaces*** in your home. I mean, the closets probably aren't exactly the first place you envision investing time and money when you move into a new space. We get it. Here's the thing, though—our small-space makeovers make every single day more fun!

There's something to be said for a bright and organized closet, a freshly painted bathroom, and the perfect storage piece for your entryway. Small-space solutions do double duty by being both beautiful and functional.

In our homes, one motto we strive to live by is "no wasted space." Every hallway, closet, and nook can have a purpose and design of its own! My favorite part about small-space projects is that most of them can happen in a weekend . . . instant gratification!

# BATHROOMS

Is your bathroom filled with messy clutter all over the sink? Damp towels draped here and there? Wall colors that just don't feel like you? This doesn't sound like a place you'd choose to retreat to. Nor does it sound like a place you'd be excited to get ready in. The bathroom is one space in our homes where we prep for the workday or a night out. Or if we've had a long day we might retreat to our bathroom for a long bubble bath with a good book (and maybe a glass of wine). You want this space to feel comfortable, not cluttered or stressful. Let's take some time to explore how to make our bathrooms into spaces we love.

### OPEN UP YOUR SPACE

So often bathrooms can feel cramped. Yes, organization and storage solutions can help, but it is also a good idea to think of ways to visually open up the space and make it feel bigger. If your bathroom has tall ceilings, find a few creative ways to draw the eye up, showing off the space. Consider adding white to the room. You could paint the walls, floors, or wood cabinets. If your budget allows, you could add white tiles to the floor or one wall, or you could change out a dingy sink for a new, pretty one.

## FOCUS ON WALL DÉCOR

It's important to choose wall décor in your bathroom that can stand up to moisture. As cute as they are, framed photos and art are not good options as they can wrinkle. Canvas wall art is a great option. Another fun idea is to create a grouping of smaller pieces, like these painted hand mirrors. Grouping small collections is a great way to make a statement with wall space!

## STORAGE IS EVERYTHING

Running a little low on storage in your bathroom? Create a beautiful and functional storage shelf! This shelf was a flea market find that was easily restyled with a few coats of spray paint and some metal locker baskets. The shelf is useful for storing extra towels, toiletries, and bath products. This method can seriously stretch the storage possibilities in your small space. All you need is one open wall!

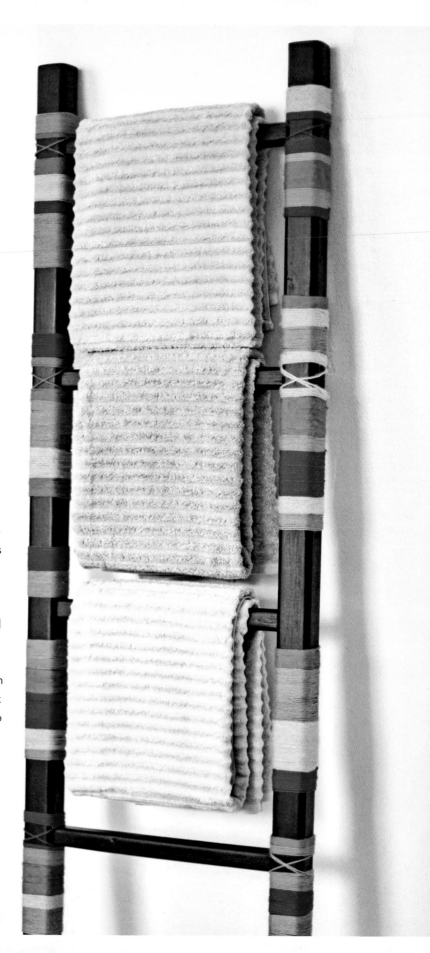

*d.i.y.*

## COLORFUL TEAK
## TOWEL RACK

Add a pop of color to your
bathroom with this super easy
idea. Use any color yarn that
fits your space.

**SUPPLIES**
wooden ladder
black latex paint
paintbrush
5 colors of yarn

**1.** Paint the ladder with 2 coats of the
black latex paint and let dry.

**2.** Starting at the top of the ladder, tie
one color of yarn around one of the legs
(with the knot in the back) and begin to
wrap the yarn around the leg. Tie a new
color of yarn onto that string to switch
colors (try to stagger the placement and
widths of the colors for variety).

**3.** At the end of a section, tie your yarn
end onto one of the strands on the back
of the leg out of sight. (When you get to
a rung, you can skip it and start a new
section after the rung, or you can make
a crisscross across the rung and keep
going).

## SHOWER CURTAIN

Make your own shower curtain to give your bathroom some extra vibes!

To start, use a paintbrush or object to stamp a design all over your shower curtain.

You can create a clustered pattern by stamping more toward the bottom of the curtain and stamp the pattern less toward the top.

To finish, allow to fully dry (check your paint bottle) before use.

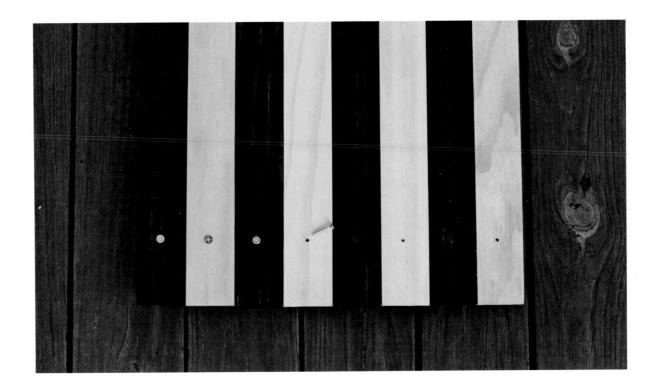

# BUBBLE BATH SHELF

If you have a bathtub, chances are you've used it to relax in a bubble bath after a long day. Am I right? Here's an easy project to create a cute shelf to hold your book, glass of wine, or whatever you need to unwind.

**1.** Stain the 8 (36-inch) wood pieces for the base of the shelf. We used a black (ebony) stain and a white stain. You can also stain the other two pieces of wood (these are for the bottom edges).

**2.** Glue the bottom two pieces to each end of the shelf.

**3.** For extra stability and to add a little shine add the gold screws to each end as well.

### SUPPLIES

8 (1½-by-½-by-36–inch) wood pieces (these can be longer or shorter depending on your tub size)

2 (1½-by-½-by-12–inch) wood pieces

wood stain

rags

wood glue

16 small gold screws

drill

# TOOTH-BRUSH HOLDER 9 WAYS

**TIP:** You can easily seal your design using Mod Podge or a thin coat of polyurethane.

**1.**
PAINT DIFFERENT-SIZED POLKA DOTS FOR A BUBBLE EFFECT.

**5.**
PAINT ON A COLORFUL, ABSTRACT DESIGN.

**6.**
ADD SIMPLE SYMBOLS OR PUNCTUATION MARKS IN PAINT PENS.

**3.**

USE MARKERS TO CREATE A NOTEBOOK DESIGN—COMPLETE WITH NOTES OR DOODLES!

*good morning + good Night !!!*

**4.**

ADD A BOLD, GRAPHIC DESIGN IN BLACK SHARPIE.

**2.**

USE COLORFUL SHARPIES OR PAINT PENS TO ADD A TRIANGLE DESIGN.

**8.**

ADD A MESSAGE. KEEP IT SIMPLE FOR MAXIMUM IMPACT.

WAKE UP!

**7.**

MIX BOLD COLORS MODELED AFTER FAVORITE FABRICS OR FASHION TRENDS.

**9.**

ADD A DESIGN THAT MIMICS YOUR FAVORITE PORCELAIN CHINA PATTERN.

# ODDS AND ENDS

It can be easy to forget the odds and ends in our homes. It's okay, just admit it: you have a messy, unorganized closet. Your entryway looks like you just moved in, even if you've lived there for years. The hallways in your home look neglected and bare. It can be easy to forget or overlook the small spaces in our lives, but these are opportunities to add color, personality, and life to our homes. Look around your house this week and notice any long forgotten corners and make a goal to tackle these spots this month. You can do it! Here are a few tips and ideas to get you started.

### SHOE STORAGE

Raise your hand if you're a little shoe obsessed. Me too! One fun idea is to have shelves custom built to store your growing collection. The shelves will save floor space, while keeping shoes in sight so you can always find the pair you're searching for!

**CLOSET COLOR CRATES**
A storage solution that's both functional and colorful is painted milk crates! These crates can be purchased on the cheap and painted with your favorite colors.

d.i.y.

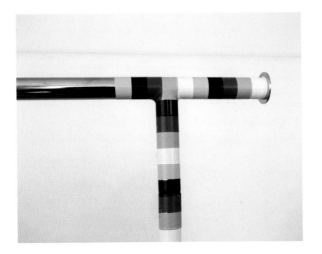

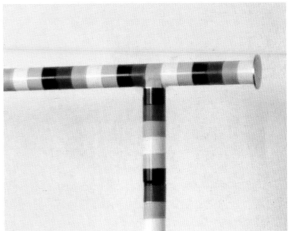

# COLORFUL CLOTHING RACK

Are your clothes overflowing out of your closet? Try embellishing a freestanding clothes rack to add color and storage space to your closet area.

**1.** Starting at the bottom of the clothing rack, wrap one color of the electrical tape around the metal pole and cut the tape.

**2.** Repeat with each color and continue that color pattern until all the surfaces of the clothing rack are covered.

**SUPPLIES**

electrical tape (several colors)

scissors

metal clothing rack

## JEWELRY DISPLAY 2 WAYS

Don't you just hate it when your necklaces and bracelets get all tangled together?

*1.* Collect a few glass bottles (liquor, wine, or soda bottles work well). Spray paint them to match your aesthetic and seal with a spray sealant. Use the bottles in your room to display your jewelry.

*2.* Another option is to attach a few mismatched knobs to a wooden board and display on a wall. Hang necklaces from the knobs to keep them organized.

*1.*

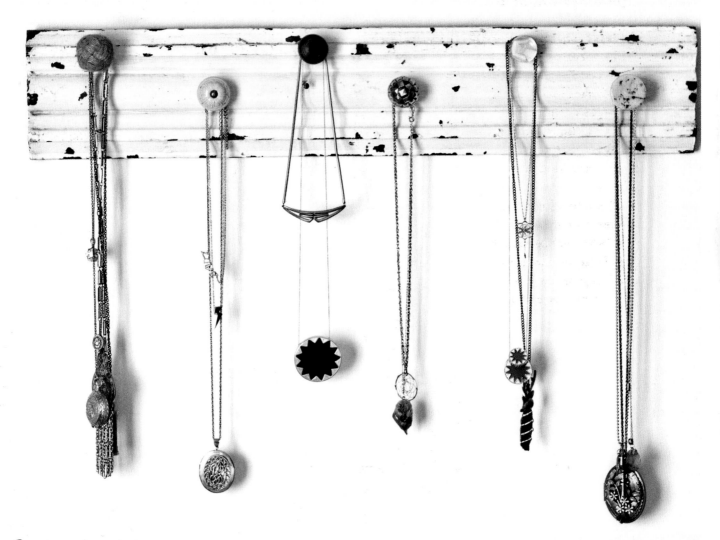

2.

d.i.y.

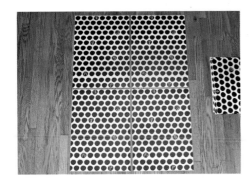

# MAKE YOUR OWN WALLPAPER

Want to add pattern to your space but you can't find wallpaper that suits your taste? Why not make your own? Here's how.

**SUPPLIES**

wallpaper paste

wallpaper squeegee

painting roller

tiled printed paper

Valspar Clear Protector

*1.* Use a design program like Photoshop or Illustrator to create a "tiled" pattern that will line up and continue with the pieces next to it as well as below and above it.

*2.* Measure the area that you intend to cover to determine how many 11-by-17-inch prints you will need.

*3.* Print at home or have a local printer create your prints.

*4.* Prepare the wall and determine if sanding, priming, or cleaning is needed.

*5.* Follow the wallpaper paste instructions to apply the paste with a roller to

the back of your print. Hang your prints starting in the top corner of your area and use a wallpaper squeegee to smooth out any bubbles.

*6.* Line up your tiled prints carefully. Move down the wall by pasting the print beneath it in place. If the paper is longer than the bottom of the wall, mark where the paper should be trimmed and cut the paper.

*7.* Continue pasting the paper until the whole wall is covered.

*8.* Once the wallpaper paste is dry, use the Clear Protector per instructions on top of the wallpaper and let it dry.

# SCARF CURTAIN

Use vintage or thrifted scarves to create a fancy curtain for your hallway. The thin fabric will allow for some light to leak through, adding color to your space.

### SUPPLIES

scissors

various scarves (enough to cover the entire window)

straight pins

needle

thread

curtain rod

**1.** Cut your scarves into the desired size of squares (they should all be the same size).

**2.** Lay out your scarf squares on the floor and arrange them in a pattern you like.

**3.** Take the top row and sew the sides of the scarves together, creating one long row. When sewing the sides of the squares, the front sides should face each other (the nice side of the seam should be facing the front when done).

**4.** Repeat with each row.

**5.** Pin all your long rows together and sew the rows together (again, the fronts should be facing each other when sewing and the nice side of the seam should be facing the front).

**6.** Once all your rows have been sewn together, fold over the top 3 inches of your curtain (fold toward the back) and sew to create an open pocket that you can put the curtain rod through.

**7.** Place the curtain rod through the top and hang your new curtain.

# DRESSER MAKEOVER

Add some personality to your entryway by giving a side table or dresser a makeover. Make your own stamp to create a truly unique piece!

**SUPPLIES**

dresser

white primer

black acrylic paint

brushes

ruler

pencil

craft foam

scissors

cardboard

**1.** Paint each side of the dresser drawers with a coat (or two, if needed) of primer. Allow to dry.

**2.** On two drawers, use a ruler to make 1-inch-wide stripes and fill in the alternating stripes with black acrylic paint.

**3.** For the other drawers, use scissors to cut the craft foam to create the design that you want to stamp and glue the foam stamp onto the cardboard backing.

**4.** Stamp the sides of the drawers with the black acrylic paint. Once all the paint has fully dried, you can put the drawers back in the dresser and it's ready for use.

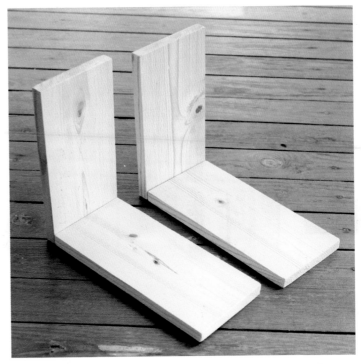

# BOOKENDS

Use any plastic toy or figurines to create your own custom bookends. These can add quite a statement to an otherwise dull bookshelf or tabletop in your hallway.

**SUPPLIES**

4 wood boards for the base

wood glue

figurines

spray primer

spray paint

spray sealer

paint

paintbrush

Krazy Glue

*1.* Buy or have boards cut that are the same length and height as your figurines. Use the wood glue to adhere the boards together and allow to fully dry.

*2.* Prime the figurines and allow to fully dry.

*3.* Spray paint the figurines and allow to fully dry.

*4.* Seal the figurines and allow to fully dry.

*5.* Paint your wood base and allow to fully dry.

*6.* Use crazy glue to adhere the figurines to the wood base frames. Once they are dry, you are ready to display your new bookends!

# PICTURE FRAMES 9 WAYS

**TIP:** Seal surfaces with Mod Podge to ensure that your designs don't smudge over time.

**1.**
COVER IN CHALKBOARD PAINT SO YOU CAN ADD MESSAGES LATER.

**5.**
COVER IN COLORFUL WASHI TAPE.

**6.**
COVER IN WALLPAPER SCRAPS OR FOUND PAPERS.

**2.**

COVER IN
A FUN FLORAL
FABRIC.

**4.**

PAINT WHITE,
THEN ADD KISSY-
LIPS IN MULTIPLE
LIPSTICK SHADES.
BE SURE TO SEAL
THIS ONE!

**3.**

GLUE ON A DESIGN
IN FOAM, THEN
SPRAY-PAINT THE
ENTIRE FRAME FOR
A RAISED DESIGN.

**7.**

PAINT METALLIC,
THEN ADD CUT
FOAM ACCENTS.

**8.**

GLUE ON A
BORDER OR
PATTERN WITH
SMALL PIECES OF
BALSA WOOD.

**9.**

ADD A BOLD
BLACK-AND-
WHITE PATTERN
WITH PAINT AND
SHARPIES.

# *Acknowledgments*

This book would not have happened without the generous help and support of Laura Gummerman, Katie Shelton, Kinsey Mhire, Janae Hardy, Doren Chapman, Lindsay Edgecombe, Camaren Subhiyah, and Julie Mazur.

Special thanks to:
- our wonderful husbands, Jeremy and Trey, for letting us tear up the houses for nearly a whole year
- Michael Martin, our favorite contractor
- our sweet friends and family for all your love and support

# *Resources*

**COVER**

**Prints**/etsy.com/shop/ashleyg
and shop.finelittleday.com
**Couches**/ThriveFurniture.com
**Lamp**/UrbanOutfitters.com

**PAGE 15**

**Floral Poster**/DebbieCarlos.com

**PAGE 20**

**Couch**/UrbanOutfitters.com
**Pillow**/Anthropologie.com
**Rug**/Target.com

**PAGE 25**

**Pillows**/SkinnylaMinx.com
**Couch**/Macys.com

**PAGE 28**

**Wicker Chair**/Amazon.com
**Pillow**/SkinnylaMinx.com
**Blanket**/WestElm.com

**PAGE 29**

**Couch**/ThriveFurniture.com
**Rug**/Target.com
**Chairs**/Amazon.com
**Pendant Lamp**/Ikea

**PAGES 36–37**

**Couch and Love Seat**/
ThriveFurniture.com
**Flokati Rug**/UrbanOutfitters.com

**PAGE 57**

**Refrigerator**/BigChill.com

**PAGE 88**

**Globe Lantern**/Young House Love for
ShadesOfLight.com

**PAGE 117**

**Capiz Pendant**/WestElm.com
**Floral Poster**/DebbieCarlos.com
**Lamp**/UrbanOutfitters.com
**Lace Curtains**/Ikea

**PAGE 123**

**Yellow Lamps**/WestElm.com
**Bedding**/UrbanOutfitters.com
**Pendleton Pillow**/
etsy.com/shop/RobinCottage

**PAGE 139**

**Magazine File**/Martha Stewart
for Avery
**Lamp**/UrbanOutfitters.com

**PAGE 141**

**Couch**/Flea Market

**PAGE 166–167**

**Acapulco Chairs**/Amazon.com
**Hammock**/etsy.com/shop/hamanica

**PAGE 171**

**Orange Chairs**/
DesignFormFurnishings.com

**PAGE 175**

**Lucite Tray**/WestElm.com

**PAGE 185**

**Custom Dog Plush**/
www.SleepyKing.net
**Daisy Lamp**/Ikea

**PAGE 210**

**Abstract Painting**/
Elizabeth Chapman (Our mom!)
melizabethchapman.blogspot.com

# *Index*